ACTIVE ASSESSMENT

Thinking Learning and Assessment in Science

STUART NAYLOR AND BRENDA KEOGH
WITH ANNE GOLDSWORTHY

 David Fulton Publishers

 Millgate House Publishers

SUPPORTED BY

 GlaxoSmithKline

The **Association** for **Science Education**

David Fulton Publishers Ltd

The Chiswick Centre, 414 Chiswick High Road, London W4 5TF

www.fultonpublishers.co.uk

www.onestopeducation.co.uk

in association with

Millgate House Publishers, Millgate House, 30 Mill Hill Lane, Sandbach,

Cheshire CW11 4PN, UK

www.millgatehouse.co.uk

First published in Great Britain by David Fulton Publishers, in
association with Millgate House Publishers, 2004
Reprinted 2005 (three times), 2006
10 9 8 7 6 5

David Fulton is a division of Granada Learning Limited, part of
ITV plc.

British Library Cataloguing in Publication Data.
A record for this book is available from the British Library.

ISBN 1 84312 145 X

Typesetting and Graphic Design by Kathyrn Stawpert
Illustrations by Ged Mitchell
CD by Angel Solutions, www.angelsolutions.co.uk

Printed and bound in Great Britain

Acknowledgments

Like any book this one draws on the ideas of colleagues who have inspired us and helped us to think creatively about assessment. Prominent amongst these are Richard Gunstone and Richard White, who helped us to understand the connection between assessment and learning and provided a firm foundation on which we could build. Without their book, Probing Understanding (Falmer, 1992), we doubt whether this book would have been written.

Our illustrator, Ged Mitchell, provides the visual resource to accompany the text. As well as filling our walls with his paintings it is a pleasure to fill our books with his images.

Our chief magician and graphic designer, Kathryn Stawpert, has the enviable skill of bringing a page of text to life and extending our ideas of what is possible to do with a book. This book would be much less engaging without her creative influence.

The CD to accompany the book has been developed by Angel Solutions. With their extensive experience of working with educational organizations and understanding of educational issues, they were the ideal partner for translating parts of the publication into electronic form.

Thanks also to:

Dave Kellam and Tom Murphy VII for permission to use their custom designed fonts and Greenstreet Software Ltd

www.greenstreetsoftware.com

Contents

PART 1

Introduction	3
Assessment and learning	5
Assessment and teaching	9
Assessment and recording	13
Creating the right environment	15

PART 2

Examples of active assessment strategies	19

PART 3

References and bibliography	149
Related titles of interest	151

Index

of assessement techniques
and examples used

Page No	Assessment Technique	Activity 1	Activity 2	Additional Resources on CD
19	Card sort	Plant parts	Energy	
23	Cartoon strip sequence	Daytime shadows	Gas exchange	Blank worksheet
27	Classifying and grouping	Seed sort	Sorting materials-Solids, liquids and gases	
31	Concept cartoons	Muscles	Forces and pressure	With blank speech bubbles
35	Concept maps	Weather	Electric circuits	Incomplete concept map
39	Concept sentences	Melting and dissolving	Acids and alkalis	
43	Consumer report	Is it waterproof?	Conductors - Electrical and thermal	
47	Data: analysing data	Melting ice	Life in a compost heap	
51	Data: completing or creating tables	Testing threads	Enzyme activity	
55	Deliberate mistakes	Stretching tights	Germinating seeds	
59	Diary entries for a scientist	What are frogs?	Flat or round Earth?	Incomplete version
63	Drawings and annotated drawings	Movement of the sun	How we see	Examples without annotations
67	Games	Skeleton game	Snakes and ladders	Resources for the games

Page No	Assessment Technique	Activity 1	Activity 2	Additional Resources on CD
71	**Graphic organisers: compare and contrast**	Bird and bat	Photosynthesis and respiration	**Blank grids**
75	**Graphic organisers: reasoning by analogy**	Whale and submarine	Electric circuit and central heating	**Blank grids**
79	**Graphic organisers: whole - parts relationship**	Eagle	Circulatory system	**Blank grids**
83	**Generating a set of instructions**	Growing seeds	Separating Rock salt	
87	**KWL grids**	Teeth	Light	**Blank grid**
91	**Writing a letter**	Fred Bear's coat	Disposable cup	
95	**Making a list**	Push and pull walk	Light and sound comparison	**Pull list**
99	**Matching exercises**	Flower parts	Rock bingo	**Bingo cards**
103	**News reports**	Vanishing sugar - dissolving	Cosmic storm - Electron movement in metals	**Blank layout**
107	**Odd one out**	Light sources	Changes - physical and chemical	**Blank grid**
111	**Posters**	How cats see in the dark	Light bulb	**Poster framework**
115	**Predict, observe, explain**	Floating and sinking	Electric circuit	
119	**Questions: generating questions**	Sound and music	Van Helmont's experiment	**Question stems**
123	**Questions: responding to questions**	Light and shadows	Ready, steady cook! - Reversible and non-reversible change	
127	**Sales pitch or advertisement**	A home for a frog	Favourite metal	
131	**Sequencing: statements, pictures and ideas**	Change of state	Energy transfer	
135	**Thought experiments**	Falling stone	Predator-prey interaction	
139	**True-False statements**	Pushes and pulls	Earth and beyond	
143	**Word definitions**	Forces	Food chains	

PART 1

Introduction 3

Assessment and learning 5

Assessment and teaching 9

Assessment and recording 13

Creating the right environment 15

Introduction

Active assessment in science

Part of a teacher's job is to assess pupils. It's included in the job description. However, even if assessment were not a requirement, good teachers would continue to assess pupils. They know that assessment informs them about what pupils have learnt, indicates what pupils may be finding difficult and helps them to adjust their teaching to maximise pupils' learning.

This book is about active assessment in science in primary and secondary schools. It is about how thinking, learning and assessment can be linked together in a creative and integrated fashion, so that thinking promotes learning, learning enables assessment to take place and assessment acts as a stimulus to both thinking and learning. That may sound ambitious, but we believe that good teachers already do this. This book draws on this good practice to provide real guidance on how to go about it.

Building on research

This book builds on recent research and guidance on assessment, especially that produced by Black and Wiliam (1998), the Assessment Reform Group (1999) and Black et al. (2002). These publications have been highly influential in raising the profile of assessment and in offering guidance on how assessment can be made more effective. The principles that they put forward underpin our writing. We have

> **"Thinking, learning and assessment can be linked together in a creative and integrated fashion."**

3

" assessment acts as a stimulus to both
thinking and learning. **"**

translated these principles into practical strategies that can be used in the classroom during science lessons.

Assessment and learning: research into practice

Most of the book is therefore taken up with descriptions of practical strategies for assessment and learning in science. Each strategy is described in terms of:

■ what it is

■ how teachers can use it

■ how it can help with assessment

■ how it can help with learning

We have also provided illustrations of what these strategies might look like in the classroom, set in the context of different areas of science. A matrix in Part 3 provides an overview of the

strategies and the contexts in which they are set. For each strategy there are two illustrations. The first illustration is likely to be suitable for younger learners while the second illustration is for older learners. These illustrations are also provided separately on the accompanying CD ROM. The CD also provides additional resources and allows you to use a data projector to share the activity with the whole class and to interact with the text using the normal interactive white board facilities (such as highlighting).

If you are intending to improve your understanding and practice in assessment in science and would welcome guidance on how to make it more creative and more effective, then this is the book for you.

Assessment and learning

Assessment makes a difference

Assessment makes a difference to learning. There is ample evidence to support that statement, summarised most effectively by Black and Wiliam (1998) in their extensive review of published research. It can make a positive difference when learners are actively involved in their own learning, when assessment is an integral part of the learning experience and when assessment enhances self esteem and motivation.

It can also make a negative difference. Assessment can inhibit learning when, for example, teachers emphasise quantity or presentation of work rather than learning, grading work rather than giving advice for improvements and comparisons between learners which demoralise the least successful (Assessment Reform Group, 1999).

Learning through assessment

In generating the assessment activities in this book our intention has been to take account of current research into learning in science. We recognise that learners do not simply receive knowledge from a teacher but that they have to construct their own understanding of scientific concepts. They build on and modify their existing ideas in the process and are influenced by social interaction.

All the assessment activities described in this book provide opportunities for

> **"All the assessment activities described in the book provide opportunities for learning as well as for assessment."**

5

learning as well as for assessment. Assessment and learning are integrated in each activity. As Black and Wiliam put it (1998:12), "A good test can be a learning as well as a testing occasion". The activities in the book provide opportunities for learners to share their ideas in such a way that sharing provides a context and a purpose for finding out more about their ideas. From the teacher's perspective, sharing ideas is an opportunity for assessment by gaining access to the learners' ideas. From the learner's perspective, sharing ideas is a normal and purposeful part of their learning rather than a formal assessment.

Collaboration in assessment and individual assessment

Discussion and argument about scientific ideas play a vital role in thinking about and learning science. Scientific argument helps learners to clarify their thinking, to justify their ideas using evidence and reasoning, to evaluate evidence and to base conclusions on evidence rather than on feelings. For this reason, most of the assessment activities described in this book are best carried out in small groups rather than being used for individual assessment. All of the assessment activities provide opportunities for learners to share, discuss, evaluate, re-interpret and modify their ideas. In principle this kind of dialogue can happen between individual learners and the teacher, but the opportunities to do this are very limited. Small group discussions can involve everyone, so there is maximum opportunity to use discussion to enhance learning.

Teachers also need to make assessment judgements about individuals. Although learners may have worked collaboratively on an activity, in most cases it is possible to follow up group discussion with some

> **66** ...assessment activities provide opportunities for learners to share, discuss, evaluate, re-interpret and modify their ideas. **99**

individual work. This enables teachers to assess individual learners, although it is surprising how much information teachers can get about individuals from the outcome of group discussions. Guidance on how assessment can be individualised is given throughout the book.

Assessment for learning

The purpose of this book is to provide guidance for teachers, which helps them to actively involve learners in their learning, to integrate assessment as part of productive learning experiences, and to provide opportunities for assessment which enhance motivation and self esteem. In other words, to use assessment as a tool for learning.

You will find that each of the assessment activities is:

- developmental - they provide a stimulus for developing ideas further

- purposeful - they create a sense of purpose for further activity

- collaborative - they provide opportunities for debate and social construction of ideas

- seamless - with no boundary between assessment and learning.

Assessment and teaching

Assessment makes a difference

Assessment is most productive when teachers use the results of assessment to adjust their teaching (Assessment Reform Group, 1999). Many teachers are committed to the principle of using assessment for finding out the learners' ideas, then helping them to build new understanding by modifying their original ideas.

However, there are real practical difficulties when it comes to putting this principle into practice in teaching. The sizes of most classes and the range of ideas likely to be found in a typical class make it impossible to provide a range of different activities in response to the learner's individual learning needs. Teachers also have to be cautious in how they approach finding out the learners' ideas in order to avoid any risk of this being counterproductive. Learners will naturally feel discouraged if the outcome of finding out their ideas is generally to be told that their ideas are wrong!

> **"Assessment is most productive when teachers use the results of assessment to adjust their teaching."**

Putting principles into practice

These difficulties point to the need for a different approach to assessment activities, where the sense of purpose for the learner is individualised rather than the activity itself. It is possible to provide similar activities for everyone in a class and to create an individual sense of purpose that will vary according to each learner's starting

> **❝** All the assessment activities described in the book
> attempt to integrate assessment and teaching. **❞**

point. For example, if you set up an activity for learners to generate questions about a topic, they are all engaged in the same activity but the questions that they raise depend on their individual ideas. From the teacher's perspective there is only the one activity to manage; from the learner's perspective the activity is directly related to their individual level of understanding.

Similarly, the class discussion following an activity such as Card Sort or True-False statements can identify areas of uncertainty where the class as a whole fails to reach agreement. These areas can be common to the class, even though the level of understanding of individuals will vary. Identifying areas of uncertainty leads on to further work (such as practical investigation or researching secondary sources) which individual learners see as directly related to their personal learning agenda. From the teacher's

perspective it is possible to provide the same learning opportunities to the class as a whole; from the learner's perspective the support for finding out more in certain areas is directly related to their personal learning needs.

Integrating assessment and teaching

All the assessment activities described in this book attempt to integrate assessment and teaching. To use White and Gunstone's words (1992: 39), "Good testing devices are good teaching devices". Just as we have tried to make assessment and learning 'seamless', we have also attempted to do the same with assessment and teaching so that it is not possible to say where one ends and the other begins. In each of the various sections you will therefore find:

- assessment techniques which also act as worthwhile starting points for learning, so that learners will not view the activities as formal assessment

- ideas, guidance and resources which help to provide a context and purpose for further activity

- opportunities for collaborative activities which promote discussion and argument and support learners in modifying and developing their ideas

- activities which help to create an individual sense of purpose that will vary according to each learner's starting point.

Planning for assessment

Good assessment doesn't just happen. Like good teaching, good assessment needs to be planned. You will need to consider:

- what your intentions are

- what strategy will be suitable for the topic that you are teaching

- what the learner's previous experience is

- what advance preparation you need to do

- what resources you may need and what may go wrong when you actually do this in the classroom.

You will know when you get it right because your teaching will be more stimulating, learners will be more motivated and learning will be more successful.

11

Assessment and recording

The purpose of recording

There can be several reasons for learners to record their work including:

- clarifying their ideas through producing a record, which may be oral, written or pictorial

- helping them to recognise what learning has occurred, especially if they make some kind of record early in an activity to compare with their understanding later in the activity

- using the record for revision later in the year

- producing a permanent record that teachers can use for assessment

- producing a record for accountability purposes, such as when the headteacher wishes to monitor or evaluate a teacher's work.

Making the links

Where teachers use recording well it can make a valuable contribution to assessment and learning. There is considerable overlap between productive assessment and recording. Assessment strategies can function as a record of learners' work; recording can produce tangible evidence which can be used for assessment. The activities in this book therefore include a range of strategies for recording learners' work which require engagement in the learning process and which simultaneously provide a basis for assessment.

> " Where teachers use recording well it can make a valuable contribution to assessment and learning. "

13

> *What the teacher sees is a learning activity which simultaneously provides a tangible record and an opportunity for assessment.*

For example, the basis for the Sales Pitch or Advertisement activity (page 127) is to create something which will advertise an object, event or process, such as advertising a home for a frog. In order to engage in the activity it is necessary for learners to find out more about where and how frogs live so that they can make a judgement about what kind of home would be most suitable. Then they have to apply their learning to invent a suitable advertisement that would appeal to homeless frogs. The outcome of the activity is a tangible record - such as a poster or collage - which gives an indication of what they have found out about frogs and frog habitats. Teachers can use this record for assessment. What learners experience is a creative and engaging learning activity. What the teacher sees is a learning activity which simultaneously provides a tangible record and an opportunity for assessment.

Creating opportunities for recording

Not all of the activities in the book directly result in a record of learners' work, though most of them do. Where producing a record is not built into the assessment strategy it is usually possible to include some kind of recording if this is seen as desirable. For example, a Card Sort (page 19) could lead to the production of two grids, one showing 'Our ideas at the start' and the other showing 'Our ideas when we finished'; a Concept Map (page 35) created using moveable cards can be bluetacked into position and photocopied; a Thought Experiment (page 135) could lead to a picture or short piece of writing to indicate what result is predicted and why. Not all of these records will be written records, and this helps to avoid the boredom factor which can so easily set in when learners are asked to put pen to paper.

14

Creating the right environment

The impact of the teacher

This book provides guidance on alternative assessment strategies for teachers of science. However, in order to be effective in assessment teachers need to do more than use suitable strategies. Assessment and learning will be most effective when teachers also create a productive classroom climate and promote relevant learning and teaching styles. These will determine how readily learners engage with the various activities, how fully they engage and how willing they are to share their ideas. Without proper engagement any assessment activity is likely to be inaccurate as an assessment strategy and ineffective as a learning experience. Conversely, if learners are fully engaged with the activity then they will be more motivated, they will give a more accurate indication of their level of achievement and they will learn more.

> **"...the learning environment which a teacher creates has a profound impact on the success of the assessment strategies used."**

For example, learners may find it difficult to generate questions as part of assessment for learning (see Generating Questions, page 119) if during other parts of a lesson they are discouraged from asking questions. They are unlikely to think creatively about scientific problems (see Diary Entries for a Scientist, page 59, or Thought Experiments, page 135) if creative thinking is not usually encouraged by the teacher. They may struggle to work collaboratively in an activity if the usual arrangement is for them to work individually. In this way the learning environment which a teacher creates has a profound impact on the success of the assessment strategies used.

> **"** ... if learners are fully engaged with the activity
> then they will be more motivated. **"**

Creating a climate for learning and assessment

Some suggestions for how teachers can create the type of learning environment which will enable them to make best use of assessment for learning are listed below. There will be other suggestions that could be added to the list, but these will be enough to make a real difference to learning, teaching and assessment.

- Make sure that learners are actively engaged in the learning process

- Ensure that all learners' ideas are valued

- Explore incorrect ideas rather than dismiss them

- Don't evaluate their ideas - get them to do this

- Use thinking questions rather than recall questions

- Allow plenty of thinking time when you ask learners to think

- Encourage learners to argue about science and to collaborate in developing their ideas

- Get learners to justify their ideas and to evaluate the evidence for or against alternative viewpoints

- Use strategies to involve all the class in dialogue rather than just some of them

- Try to give learners choices rather than making all the decisions for them

- Provide feedback which identifies how learners can improve and which is a stimulus to further thinking.

PART 2

Examples of active
assessment strategies

Card sort

What is a card sort?

A card sort is an activity in which the learners are given cards with statements or pictures on them. They use the information on the cards to sort the cards into different groups.

How can you use card sorts?

You will need to prepare cards with suitable statements, probably with pictures as well as statements for younger or less fluent readers. Some of the statements can be straightforward while others can be more challenging. It is particularly helpful to include common misconceptions or areas of difficulty in the statements.

The simplest way to do a card sort is for small groups to discuss the statements and sort the cards into piles according to whether they agree or disagree with the statements. The groups should aim to reach consensus if possible. A third category of 'It depends on . . .' can be a useful addition.

When the cards have been sorted you can get feedback about each statement across the whole class. Groups should be asked to justify the reasons for their decisions so that the strength of evidence to support individual statements can be evaluated. The areas of disagreement or uncertainty tend to be the ones worth spending more time on. These can then be the focus for the next part of the lesson, in which the learners need to find out more about these aspects of the topic.

19

> " As the learners discuss
> their ideas they may well
> change their ideas. "

How can card sorts help with assessment?

This can be an individual assessment activity. However it is much more valuable as a small group activity where the learners have to discuss each statement and reach consensus in order to decide what to do with the card. As a group activity you can still use card sorts for assessment since they identify areas of uncertainty where learning needs to be consolidated. Usually, where all the learners agree they are thinking along the right lines.

How can card sorts help with learning?

As the learners discuss their ideas they may well change their ideas. Having to justify their own ideas, consider other learners' views and evaluate the available evidence will challenge their thinking and may lead them to change their views. This process of scientific argument is an important part of learning in science. For example, the statement that all plants have seeds (see activity) can only be resolved when learners have considered questions such as "Do I know of any plants that don't have seeds?" and "Might there be plants that I don't know about that don't have seeds?"

Identifying areas of disagreement or uncertainty sets a learning agenda for the learners. This is a useful way of building on their ideas and developing them further. As the learners make their ideas public you don't need to take on a judgmental role as the teacher. Instead you can emphasise your role in helping them to develop their ideas.

Plant Parts

ALL PLANTS HAVE:

ROOTS	SPIKES
BRANCHES	LEAVES
BULBS	SEEDS
FLOWERS	STEMS
BUDS	A TOP AND A BOTTOM

A BACK AND A FRONT

21

Energy

Sort these statements into:

AGREE, DISAGREE or IT DEPENDS ON . . .

FOOD GIVES YOU ENERGY	ENERGY GIVES YOU STRENGTH
WE USE A LOT OF ENERGY IN RUNNING	WHEN WE FEEL TIRED WE DON'T HAVE MUCH ENERGY
THERE IS ENERGY IN PETROL	THERE ARE LOTS OF DIFFERENT KINDS OF ENERGY
CARS USE ENERGY WHEN THEY GO FAST	NUCLEAR POWER PLANTS MANUFACTURE ENERGY
ENERGY IS NOT CREATED OR DESTROYED	THE WORLD IS RUNNING OUT OF ENERGY
GLOBAL WARMING IS BECAUSE WE ARE USING TOO MUCH ENERGY	PLANTS GET ENERGY FROM THE SUN
ENERGY IS FORCE	ENERGY IS POWER

WE GET ENERGY FROM THE SUN WHEN WE SUNBATHE

22

Cartoon strip sequence

What are cartoon strip sequences?

A cartoon strip sequence is a series of cartoon-style pictures that shows a sequence of events. The pictures are likely to be labelled or annotated. The purpose of using a cartoon strip sequence is to explore the learners' ideas about the sequence of events in a scientific process or series of processes.

How can you use cartoon strip sequences?

The way that you use these will depend on the age and maturity of the learners. You might have a sequence of several empty boxes in which the learners draw a picture of each event and write a brief description for each picture. For example, you might ask learners to show the various stages of where a loaf of bread comes from (see Nuffield Primary Science, 1993 for more detail). Less fluent writers might draw a sequence of pictures without any written description, or they might select suitable words or phrases from a word bank to add to their pictures. The section on Sequencing (page 131) gives further ideas.

Cartoon strip sequences could be used at the start of an enquiry to invite the learners to share their initial ideas or to make predictions about what they think will happen. For example, they might draw what they expect for the main stages in the life cycle of a bean, or they might draw a series of pictures to show how they think day and night occur. Working in small groups to produce a set of pictures, then sharing these across the whole class, will produce a set of possibilities that can then be explored in the follow up activity involving growing beans in the classroom or studying models of the solar system.

23

... cartoon strip sequences
provide evidence of the
nature and depth of the
learners' understanding.

How can cartoon strip sequences help with assessment?

The cartoon strip sequences provide evidence of the nature and depth of the learners' understanding. You can use these for assessment by reviewing the sequences that the learners produce and making a judgement about the accuracy of their ideas. If you wish to use them for assessment of individuals you can provide time for group discussion and then have individuals produce their own cartoon strip sequence.

How can cartoon strip sequences help with learning?

As the learners discuss their ideas for the sequence they will clarify their ideas, think about what evidence they have to support their ideas and identify areas of uncertainty. This helps to create a sense of purpose for them in the follow-up activity. It can help to focus their observations or research since they know what they want to learn about. It can also enable the teacher to make a judgement about which aspects of the topic to target in order to develop the learners' ideas most effectively.

Daytime Shadows

25

Gas Exchange

26

Classifying and grouping

What is classifying and grouping?

Classifying and grouping are closely related. Classifying involves using criteria to decide which group something belongs to; grouping usually starts one stage earlier, with learners putting things into groups without the criteria being fixed in advance. A useful extension of classifying is constructing keys to classify a set of objects. The best way to understand how keys work is to construct one.

How can you use classifying and grouping?

Classifying and grouping can be carried out with real objects, pictures, drawings, statements or a combination of text and pictures. Having tangible objects that learners can move around is helpful; similarly drawings or pictures are helpful for all learners, not just less fluent readers.

Classifying and grouping can be an individual activity. However, it is more valuable as a small group activity where the learners have to discuss each possibility and try to reach consensus in order to decide what it is or in which group it should go.

How can classifying and grouping help with assessment?

You can use classifying and grouping for assessment by reviewing the judgements that the learners make and the criteria that they use to make these judgements. These will give you information about the level of understanding that the learners have. Assessment of individuals can involve each learner explaining the criteria used to make classification judgements following a group discussion of the general principles involved. After the groups have engaged in the activity you can get feedback to find out what level of agreement there is across the whole class. The areas of disagreement or uncertainty help to set a learning agenda. They become the focus for the next activity, in which learners find out more about these areas.

How can classifying and grouping help with learning?

Classifying and grouping both involve learners in making judgements. They need to think about definitions, to compare and contrast, to look for evidence (e.g. Does a fire breathe?) and to apply their ideas. Critical thinking is involved, and in some cases further investigation or enquiry will be necessary.

Scientific argument involves justifying their own ideas, considering other learners' views and reviewing what evidence is available. This is an important part of their learning and may well lead them to change their ideas. It is especially useful to realise that the world doesn't fit neatly into categories that we have invented. Real life is more complex than that. For most of the common categories that we use in science there are examples of things which lie on the boundaries (e.g. shaving foam and hair gel are not easy to classify as solid, liquid or gas). Discussing these will challenge learners' ideas, and should help learners to realise that some things are difficult to classify because they may have attributes from more than one category.

NB In the seed activity it is helpful if you keep several of each kind of seed sellotaped to the outside of its packet so that you know what they are.

Seed Sort

All the seeds have fallen out of their packets and got mixed up in the drawer. They need to be sorted out again.

1 How many different kinds of seeds are there ?

2 Can you find a way to put the seeds into groups based on what they look like (e.g. long, fat, wrinkly seeds)?

3 Try to draw a branching diagram to separate the different groups.

4 Can you identify the individual seeds if you have a written description?

Sorting Materials

Can you fill in the table to show whether each substance is a solid, liquid or gas?

If possible, look closely at samples of the materials to help you to decide.

SUBSTANCE	SOLID	LIQUID	GAS
Milk			
Shaving Foam			
Air			
Sand			
Jelly			
Hair Gel			
Concrete			
Grease			
Steam			
Oxygen			
Glue			

© S Naylor, B Keogh, A Goldsworthy (2004)

30

Concept cartoons

What are concept cartoons?

A concept cartoon is a kind of visual argument. It shows an everyday situation in which characters are expressing different views about what is happening. It uses a cartoon-style format with conversations in speech bubbles.

How can you use concept cartoons?

Concept cartoons can be used in a variety of formats, including photocopiable handouts, overhead transparencies, posters or through a dataprojector. Although they can be used with individuals they are more effective as a group activity. They rapidly generate discussion and argument about the alternative possibilities. This provides an ideal basis for some kind of scientific enquiry to find out more about the situation.

They can be used in class, for homework, for classroom display or in less formal learning situations. In class they would normally be the starting point for a small group discussion (3-4 learners). One way to use them for homework is to invite learners to consider the concept cartoon at home and decide what they think, and possibly what their family members think, about the ideas in the concept cartoon.

They can be used at the start of a topic or part way through to elicit the learners' ideas, identify their areas of uncertainty and then build on these in some kind of enquiry or investigation. They can be used at the end of a topic to review and consolidate learning by applying learning in novel situations.

How can concept cartoons help with assessment?

Concept cartoons can be used for individual or group assessment. As a group activity they are highly effective at eliciting the learners' ideas through the discussion that they generate. They can be used for more formal assessment with individuals by using them as photocopied handouts and inviting learners to indicate who they agree with in the concept cartoon and why.

How can concept cartoons help with learning?

One of the most useful aspects of concept cartoons is the way that they integrate assessment and learning. Elicitation of the learners' ideas through discussion provides a context and a purpose for finding out more about those ideas. In this way elicitation (i.e. assessment) becomes a normal and purposeful part of the whole activity rather than being separated from learning.

Concept cartoons are a motivating stimulus for scientific argument and critical thinking. They grab the learners' attention, get them arguing about scientific ideas and make it likely that they will justify their ideas and weigh up evidence to reach a conclusion.
Examples taken from Naylor and Keogh (2000).

More information is available on the web site www.conceptcartoons.com

32

Muscles

What Do YOU Think?

33

Forces & Pressure

What Do YOU Think?

© S Naylor, B Keogh (2000)

Concept maps

What are concept maps?

A concept map is a visual representation of the links between various concepts. The concepts are shown in bubbles or boxes; learners make the links between them by using arrows and words. Arrows show which way to read the links.

How can you use concept maps?

Some learners find concept maps difficult to do on their own. Producing concept maps seems better suited to some learning styles and ways of thinking than others. If you have not used concept maps before with a class then there are some basic rules that will be helpful:

- Start with a familiar and simple topic so that they understand the process before they have to tackle more difficult concepts, and try the first one with the class as a demonstration.

- Give them something tangible to move around, such as cards with the concepts written (or drawn) on them. Don't use too many words.

- Use pictures wherever possible with younger learners and less fluent readers, emphasising the importance of the links between the concepts.

- Generate a set of words or phrases for them to use in their concept maps. Try the concept map first to make sure it works! As they become familiar with the technique it can be useful to brainstorm the set of words that will be used in the concept map.
(Based on White and Gunstone, 1992).

35

How can concept maps help with assessment?

Concept mapping can be an individual or small group assessment activity which helps to clarify the learners' ideas, provides a springboard for further learning and helps to inform you about which areas are well understood and which are more problematic. They can be used for assessment by scrutinising the links that learners make between the various concepts. You can make judgements about the accuracy, complexity and comprehensiveness of the links that they make. Links can be written in for learners who do not have well-developed writing skills. You can use them at the start of a topic to elicit the ideas that learners are bringing to the topic, or at the end to help you identify what learning has occurred. In either case the purpose is to show not just what learners know but what they understand about the links between the various concepts.

How can concept maps help with learning?

Using a concept map at the beginning of a topic and again at the end can enable learners to reflect on their own knowledge and identify how much and how well they have learnt. They are especially valuable as a small group activity in which learners have to try to reach a shared understanding of the relationship between the different concepts. This collaborative activity usually generates serious discussion, and the fact that there is no single right answer makes it possible to involve all learners in the discussion.

The examples are based on Sizmur (1994) and Adamczyk, Willson and Williams (1994). They can be used to illustrate concept maps or challenge learners' ideas. The same examples are on the CD with and without the linking arrows.

Weather

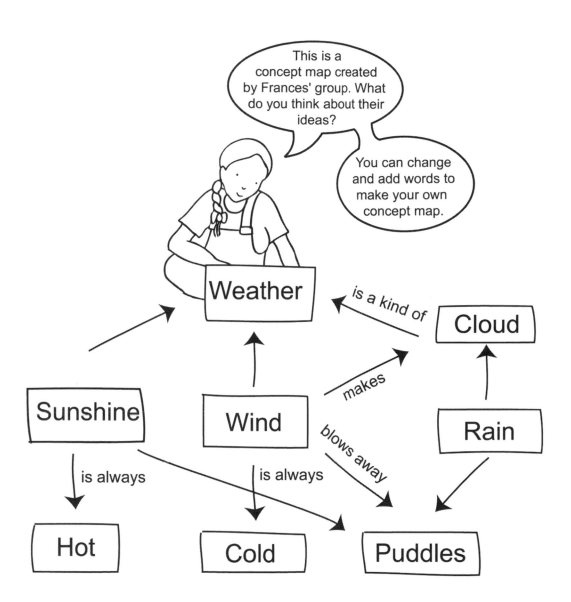

Electric Circuits

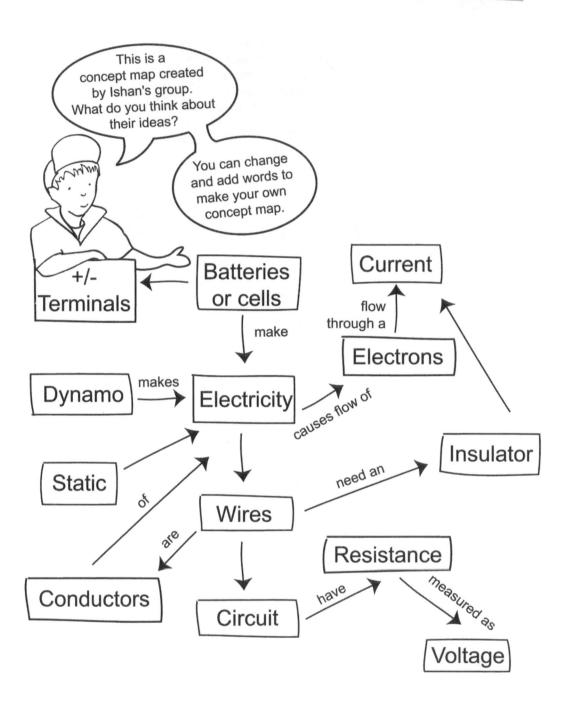

38

Concept sentences

What are concept sentences?

Learners are provided with key words or pictures on cards. These are used with words of their own choosing to form sentences about a concept or topic. When words are used it is more effective to minimise the number of nouns provided.

How can you use concept sentences?

You can ask learners to use specific words in a sentence or let them choose from a selection of words. The same words can be used several times to form new sentences. The nature and number of words that you give them will affect the level of demand of the activity. Concept sentences are best used with a group to generate discussion about the concepts. They can be used at any stage of the lesson, or group of lessons, either to raise awareness about ideas, to consolidate learning or to assess ideas.

If your class has not used concept sentences before then the following advice will be helpful:

- Start with a simple topic so that they get to understand the process before they tackle more difficult concepts or complex sentences.

- Do the first one with the class as a demonstration - e.g. on an overhead projector, using small pieces of acetate that you move around.

- Give them something tangible to move around, such as cards with the words written (or drawn) on them.

39

- You can provide pictures for the missing nouns to support younger learners and learners with learning difficulties.

- You can write the additional words for learners with limited writing skills.

- Emphasise the importance of writing interesting sentences.

- As they become familiar with the technique, the class could brainstorm the set of words that will be used in the concept sentences.

How can concept sentences help with assessment?

Concept sentences can be used for individual or group assessment. The sentences that the learners create can reveal a lot about their understanding and their creativity. If individual assessment data is needed they can be asked to create a sentence on their own using a related set of words or pictures after a group discussion.

How can concept sentences help with learning?

There is a strong link between this activity and the development of literacy skills. To create the sentences, learners need to explore each other's ideas and think about how their ideas might be expressed before the sentences can be constructed. Their sentences help them to link together words and ideas in a systematic way. The concept sentences can act as a stimulus to further research, particularly if new scientific vocabulary is being introduced.

Melting & Dissolving

Sara made a sentence using the cards below.

Do you agree with her ideas?

You can change her sentence if you want to. Make some sentences of your own. You can use the words as many times as you like.

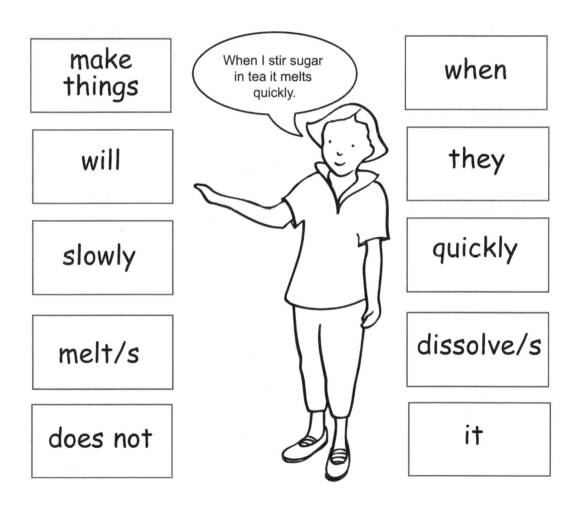

© S Naylor, B Keogh, A Goldsworthy (2004)

Acids & Alkalis

Leon made a sentence using the cards. Do you agree with his ideas?

You can change his sentence if you want to. Make some sentences of your own. You can use the words as many times as you like.

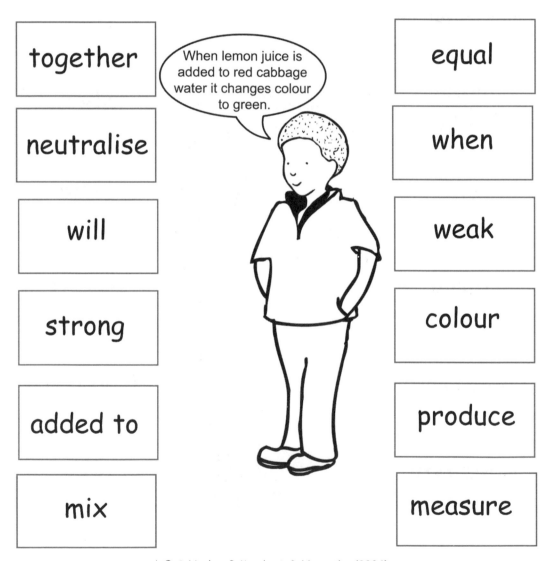

together

neutralise

will

strong

added to

mix

When lemon juice is added to red cabbage water it changes colour to green.

equal

when

weak

colour

produce

measure

Consumer report

What are consumer reports?

A consumer report is a report of a science investigation, written as though it is a
report on a set of products for a consumer magazine. It will include some kind of
evaluation of the things being studied against specific criteria.

How can you use consumer reports?

The main difference between a consumer report and any other science
investigation is the way that you set the scene. In order to generate a consumer
report it is necessary for the learners to have a clear purpose to find out more
about the items being investigated. This means that you need to do some
creative thinking about how to create a meaningful context in which the report
will be produced. Ideally the investigation will be one which is within your
scheme of work for the class anyway.

This type of investigation will normally be a group activity. It lends itself to
dividing up the investigation across a class, so that each group works on a
slightly different aspect. It could be that each group tests all the 'products'
against just one or two of the criteria, or each group might test just one or two of
the 'products' against all of the criteria. Either way you will create a purpose for
the class as a whole to share their results in order to generate the complete
picture between them.

> **The consumer report format provides an alternative way of recording the outcomes of the investigation.**

How can consumer reports help with assessment?

You can use consumer reports for assessment of individuals or groups in the same way that you can use the write up of any scientific enquiry. The report gives an indication of how the learners have carried out the enquiry, what observations they have made and what conclusions they have drawn. From this you can make judgements about the suitability of the procedures used and the level of understanding that the learners have reached.

How can consumer reports help with learning?

The most important aspects of consumer reports are that they provide a meaningful context and a clear sense of purpose for an investigation. By starting with everyday situations it is possible for learners to use their everyday intuitive understanding and see the relevance of using scientific skills to develop their ideas further. The consumer report format provides an alternative way of recording the outcomes of the investigation and avoids the risk of writing about science becoming too much of a routine activity.

Is it Waterproof?

MRS LEE WANTS TO PUT A SIGN OUTSIDE HER BAKERY TO ADVERTISE HER WONDERFUL BREAD AND CAKES. SHE NEEDS A SIGN THAT WON'T RUN IN THE RAIN. SHE HAS STARTED TO DO SOME TESTS ON WHAT SHE MIGHT USE BUT SHE IS TOO BUSY BAKING TO FINISH THE TESTS.

Can you help her to finish her tests and then write a report on what you found out?

Paper	Is it waterproof?				Number of ✓
	Pencil	Wax crayon			
Plain paper					
Coloured card					
Sugar paper					
Number of ✓					

Conductors

You are designing the **electric circuit** for a new video game. Some parts of the circuit need to be **well insulated** so they must be **surrounded** by a material which is a **poor ELECTRICAL** conductor.

However, these parts also tend to get **hot**, so they must be surrounded by a material which is a **good THERMAL** conductor.

You need to find a material which is:

 a poor ELECTRICAL conductor and

 a good THERMAL conductor.

You will have to decide what is the **best** way to test them and produce a proper report of your investigation.

Data:
analysing data

What is analysing data?

When learners analyse data, they think about what the data tells them. Analysing data can involve looking for patterns and relationships, comparing the data with predictions, deciding what is important and attempting to interpret and explain the data.

How can you use analysing data?

Learners can analyse data that they have collected themselves or data that has been collected by someone else. They can use both quantitative and qualitative data. Younger learners find it easier to work with data that they have collected themselves so that they can relate it to a real experience. Older learners will be able to work with data from other sources, such as other pupils, books or the internet. For topics involving very large or very small events or time-scales, data from secondary sources may be the only data available.

Analysing data is often used at the end of a scientific enquiry to sum up what has been found out but it can also be used to begin an enquiry. For example, you might provide data about the rate at which a container of water cools down when wrapped in different fabrics. Learners could analyse the data and list things that they found surprising and suggest things that might cause difficulties in this investigation. This might help them plan their own enquiry about insulation more effectively.

47

How can analysing data help with assessment?

The outcome of analysing data can provide direct evidence about what learners understand or are having difficulty with. It can provide information about their understanding of concepts, such as explaining the different times and directions of sunrise and sunset, and can allow you to focus on specific aspects of a topic where misconceptions are likely. It can also provide information about their understanding of procedures, such as whether something seems to have gone wrong in an investigation, and can allow you to check on specific skills that you have taught recently.

How can analysing data help with learning?

Learners often see the collection of data as the end point of a scientific enquiry. They may not expect to analyse their data and consider the evidence. You can encourage them to do this and teach them how to go about it. Sometimes they will get unexpected data from an enquiry that's 'gone wrong'. They may ignore the data and pretend that it fits the expected outcome, or they may accept the data but not discuss its limitations. Analysing the data will help them to understand the importance of the evidence and come to a better understanding of the significance of their results.

Although analysing data can be an individual activity, as a group activity it provides a basis for discussion and scientific argument as the learners share their ideas and try to reach a consensus.

Melting Ice

We got some **BIG** pieces of ice and put them in different places. We waited for the ice to melt. We found out how much water collected in half an hour.

WHERE WE PUT THE ICE	HOW MUCH WATER COLLECTED
In the classroom	45 ml
In the cupboard	38 ml
Over the radiator	63 ml
In the fridge	5 ml
In the corridor	26 ml

Some of these sentences match the results? Which ones?

1 We collected most water from the ice over the radiator.

2 The ice in the classroom melted the fastest.

3 Even the ice in the fridge melted a bit.

4 We collected twice as much water above the radiator as in the classroom.

Can you make up some sentences of your own?

Try them on a partner. See if they can spot which ones match the results and which ones don't match.

© S Naylor, B Keogh, A Goldsworthy (2004)

Compost Heap

The table shows information that was collected from observing a compost heap.

	Top of heap	Just below the top	Middle of heap	Bottom of heap
Material	Grass, leaves, dead plants. Kitchen waste - lettuce, orange peel, carrots.	Grass cuttings going grey/brown.	Slimy rotting plants, sticks, twigs, some brown grass. Can't recognise kitchen waste.	Almost like soil, brown, only sticks recognisable.
Temperature	22 °C	45 °C	33 °C	26 °C
Moisture	Fairly dry	Moist and steaming	Moist	Moist
Worms	None seen	Hardly any	Lots observed	A few

Use the data in the table above to say whether the statements are definitely true, probably true, or can't tell from the data.

	Definitely	Probably	Can't tell
The hottest place in the compost heap is just below the top			
The middle of the compost heap is hotter than the edge			
You never get worms in the top part of a compost heap			
Moisture seems to help things rot in our compost heap			
You can dig the rotted compost into the garden to help things grow			
Worms are living things so they will need air to survive			
When things are rotting they seem to get hotter			
All compost heaps will behave like this one			

50

Data:

completing or creating tables or charts

What is completing or creating tables or charts?

In these activities learners are given incomplete tables or charts and some information about the missing data. They have to work out how to fill in the missing sections. Alternatively they can create a table or chart from information that you provide.

How can you use completing or creating tables or charts?

You can use creating/completing tables or charts before an investigation to remind learners of the way that tables and charts work and how they might record their data. You can use them at the end of an enquiry to focus on how data is presented and interpreted. You can use this as an individual activity but it is more likely to be suitable as a small group activity which allows alternative views to be explored and debated.

You can set up tables and charts so that learners have to extrapolate or interpolate from the data. You can get them to produce a table or chart based on information that you provide or from secondary sources, encouraging them to think of the information as clues to a puzzle. Alternatively they can be asked to make up a set of statements from their own data (for example, data about the speed of dissolving at different temperatures). They can then swap sentences with another group or pair to work out what the table or chart would look like, based on the data.

The activity can be supported by providing large sheets of paper on which the lines for the table, or axes for the graph, are already drawn. They can be encouraged to write in pencil so that they can change things easily, or construct the table or chart using post-its or sticky labels.

How can completing and creating tables or charts help with assessment?

Completing and creating tables or charts can give you insight into how well learners understand a relationship (such as enzyme activity at different temperatures) and whether they are having difficulty with a topic. It can also provide some insight into how well learners understand the scientific enquiry process and what the evidence tells them.

How can completing and creating tables or charts help with learning?

This kind of activity helps learners to understand how information can be presented and how tables and charts can be constructed. It helps them to see how tables and charts can highlight patterns, indicate anomalies and clarify relationships between different factors. If learners work in small groups then they also have the opportunity to discuss and argue about the information presented, clarifying and consolidating their ideas as they do so.

Testing Threads

SHAMEEN AND GED NEEDED TO FIND SOME REALLY STRONG THREAD TO FIX A TEAR IN THEIR TENT. THEY DID SOME TESTS ON DIFFERENT THREADS TO FIND OUT WHEN THE THREADS BROKE, BUT THEY COULDN'T ORGANISE THEIR INFORMATION.

Can you put their information in a table?

Can you use the table to produce a bar chart?

- Two of the threads were much stronger than the other three.
- They used newton meters to pull on the threads until they broke.
- The thick nylon was stronger than the cotton by 3 newtons.
- None of the threads took more than 20 newtons to break.
- They saw how many newtons it took to break each thread.
- Two of the threads they used were polyester and wool.
- The wool broke at 4 newtons.
- The thick nylon was twice as strong as the thin nylon.
- Neither polyester or wool took more than 6 newtons to break.
- The cotton broke at 15 newtons.
- The wool was the weakest and it broke at 2 newtons less than the polyester.

Enzyme Activity

The brewery is using some new yeast to make their beer. They decided to test the yeast to find out the temperature at which it works best. They measured how thick the froth was when the beer was fermenting, and that told them how quickly the yeast was working. Here is what they found out. Unfortunately they lost some of their results.

°C TEMPERATURE	THICKNESS OF THE FROTH MM
5	
10	4
15	7
20	15
25	
30	61
35	110
40	104
45	72
50	12
55	2
60	

- Draw a graph from these results.
- What do you think the missing results are?
- What do you think the temperature is when the yeast is working fastest?
- What result do you think they would get at -5 °C and 70 °C?
- Can you think of reasons to explain the pattern in the results?

© S Naylor, B Keogh, A Goldsworthy (2004)

54

Deliberate mistakes

What are deliberate mistakes?

When you use deliberate mistakes you put something which is incorrect in front of learners and get them to spot the errors.

How can you use deliberate mistakes?

Deliberate mistakes can be set within a piece of text which contains both correct and incorrect statements, incorporated into oral presentations or discussion, or included in the teacher's actions. When used with text it is best to use a text of reasonable length so that several comments can be made, such as commenting on results or describing a process like evaporation or germination. This allows you to incorporate many statements, some of which will be true and some false. Learners then scan the text and discuss the sentences with each other in pairs or small groups. They can circle or underline the sentences they think are deliberate mistakes. In discussion they can justify their choices and say why they think certain sentences may be incorrect. After teaching, learners can reflect back on the sentences that they thought were deliberate mistakes and decide whether they want to make any additions or alterations.

Deliberate mistakes can focus on understanding scientific ideas, for example, seed dispersal and germination. They can also focus on scientific processes and procedures, such as how a fair test is set up, how observations are made, how scientific equipment is used or how results are interpreted.

> **As learners try to identify deliberate mistakes they will think about and clarify their own ideas.**

How can deliberate mistakes help with assessment?

They can be used for assessment by checking how the learners respond to the deliberate mistakes, whether they notice all the mistakes and how they think mistakes should be corrected. Specific misconceptions can be targeted by building in relevant deliberate mistakes. Learners can look for deliberate mistakes individually. However, as a small group activity, ideas can be made public and developed collaboratively and judgements can be made about which ideas need to be developed further.

How can deliberate mistakes help with learning?

As learners try to identify deliberate mistakes they will think about and clarify their own ideas. This is useful as either an individual or a group activity. Discussion with others will also help them to review evidence, justify their choices, explain their thinking and reconsider their views. If the deliberate mistakes are text-based then going back to the sentences they originally selected as deliberate mistakes and making the necessary amendments will help them to recognise what they have learnt. With oral or action based deliberate mistakes you have an opportunity to highlight misconceptions, clarify uncertainties and consolidate learning through discussion.

Stretching Tights

Some children have been testing tights. Here are their results. They seem to have made some mistakes - can you spot them?

WHAT WE DID
We got 4 pairs of tights. We put a weight down one leg and measured how much they stretched.

WHAT HAPPENED
All the tights stretched different amounts. The thin blue stripey tights stretched the most. They stretched 14cm more than the shortest tights. The thickest tights didn't stretch much. They stretched 12cm less than the yellow tights. There were two pairs of blue tights and they stretched more than the pale coloured tights.

WHAT WE LEARNED
If you want tights to stretch a lot you should buy pale colours.

OUR RESULTS	
Type of tights	How much they stretched
Thin blue stripey	55 cms
Thick green ribbed	37 cms
Medium yellow	45 cms
Thin blue check	48 cms

57

Germinating Seeds

Which deliberate mistakes can you spot in the following information?

Flowering plants grow from seeds. We say a seed has germinated once the plant has started to grow leaves. Inside every seed is an embryo (baby plant). There is nothing else inside the seed.

Every seed is surrounded by a hard protective coat. This helps the seed to survive in bad weather conditions. The hard coat stops things like air and water getting into the seed.

The seed will germinate when it is warm and light. If it has water as well it will germinate faster but it mainly needs warmth and light to start it off.

The first thing that emerges from a germinating seed is something called a radicle. This turns into the root and always grows towards the ground.

Diary entries for a scientist

What are diary entries?

At their simplest diary entries can be a record of the outcomes of a scientific enquiry, written up in the form of diary entries by a scientist. Alternatively, they can be a record of a scientist's speculations about some new idea or theory, written as though they were from a scientist at the time that those ideas were current.

How can you use diary entries?

Diary entries can be used at the start of a topic to explore what learners already know about that topic and where their uncertainties lie. They can be used at the end of a topic as a creative way of helping them to reflect on and summarise their learning or to apply their learning in a new setting.

Writing a diary entry can be an individual or a small group activity. It can be a class or a homework activity. It can be a combination of these, with an initial small group brainstorming session which then leads to an individual development of those ideas as a homework activity or longer-term project.

If a class is being asked to speculate about a scientific theory then it can be helpful to have some relevant historical background to help to set the scene for the diary entries. Colleagues with historical knowledge can be helpful here, as can simple science history texts or encyclopaedias (those written for children are ideal).

59

How can diary entries help with assessment?

You can use these diary entries for assessment by making judgements about the accuracy and completeness of the ideas which the learners describe. You may also wish to comment on how creative the diary entries are, which is part of the point of using this approach to assessment. Less fluent writers might be invited to tape record their ideas as a 'captain's log', so that their ideas can be assessed rather than their writing skills.

Even though diary entries provide useful assessment information, the format can take away some of the risk of learners losing face by giving a wrong answer. If mistakes are made then the scientist can be blamed, not the learner!

How can diary entries help with learning?

Diary entries can invite learners to speculate about scientific ideas, combining creative thinking and scientific understanding. The diary format invites them to be creative in their writing as well as in their thinking. It can also help them to recognise that science is not entirely certain, especially at times when new scientific ideas are being put forward, and that the process of developing scientific theories is often erratic, lengthy and confusing. Diary entries can be linked to learning literacy skills, where the nature of diary writing might be included as part of a literacy lesson.

The examples can be used as illustrations of diaries. They could also be used as deliberate mistakes activities. There is an incomplete example on the CD.

What are Frogs?

4th March 1783

I have been studying frogs carefully, trying to decide whether they are really land or water animals.

On the one hand they have webbed feet which are perfect for swimming. They breathe through their moist skin and lay their eggs in water. They have eyes on the tops of their heads, so that when they are resting in the water their eyes are above the surface, constantly watching for flies and other creatures.

On the other hand they have lungs, which enable them to breathe on land as we do. Their hind legs have powerful muscles with which they hop from place to place. They find and seize upon worms, slugs, insects and other tasty morsels moving on the ground.

I wonder what people in the future will think about my ideas.

Flat or Round Earth

17th November 1294

A sailor has come to the Court to say that he has been six years on the longest voyage. He claims to have sailed around the world and he sees that the Earth is round, not flat. The Court feels that he is mad or lying. After all, we simply need to look outside and see that the ground is flat, not curved. Our builders use spirit levels which are flat, not banana-shaped, in order to build houses which are straight and true.

Nevertheless I find that there is a certain strange attraction in the idea. I can see how ships would disappear over the horizon if the Earth were curved, so that instead of getting smaller and smaller until they gradually disappeared they would disappear more suddenly. I can see how countries on different parts of the Earth's surface would have day and night at different times, so that when the sun is at its height here in London it may be dark midnight on another part of our Earth.

I wonder what people in the future will think about my ideas.

© S Naylor, B Keogh, A Goldsworthy (2004)

Drawings and annotated drawings

What are drawings and annotated drawings?

A drawing can be an obvious way to enable learners to express their ideas. Annotated drawings include words as well as pictures and can be a useful extension of drawings. They enable learners to include more detail than can be included in a drawing and they can also help to compensate for a lack of graphic skill in drawing their ideas.

How can you use drawings and annotated drawings?

Drawings and annotated drawings can be used at the start of a topic to get learners to predict what they think might happen, such as whether an ice balloon will float or how a seed might change as it starts to grow. They can be used part way through an activity, possibly as a record to show what learners think is happening or how they think something is happening.

For example, they might produce an annotated drawing to show what happens when various objects are placed in water. Their drawings might include some objects that "float just below the surface" or some that "sink very slowly". In this example an annotated drawing provides more detail than a simple drawing could. Similarly they could produce an annotated drawing to show what they think is happening when water evaporates from a tank of water. In this example the annotated drawing shows not just what the learners think is happening but also why they think it is happening. This can be a very useful way of representing abstract ideas.

Learners can be presented with incomplete or incorrect annotated drawings to complete or modify. Drawings and annotated drawings can be used as an individual or a small group activity. As an individual activity it can give you access to the learners' individual ideas. As a group activity it provides a basis for discussion and scientific argument as they share their ideas within the group.

How can drawings and annotated drawings help with assessment?

Drawings and annotated drawings provide a permanent record of the learners' ideas which you can assess either during or outside lesson time. They do not usually require much teacher input or management and they can allow individual learners to find their own balance between words and pictures, depending on their literacy and graphic skills and inclinations.

How can drawings and annotated drawings help with learning?

Producing drawings and annotated drawings helps to clarify the learners' ideas. As a group activity, discussion of their drawings invites them to consider what evidence is available to support their ideas and creates a sense of purpose for follow-up activities. When used at the start of a topic they can help learners to identify their own uncertainties and generate the need to find out more through the activities and resources that the teacher provides.

The examples can be used as illustrations. They could also be used as deliberate mistakes activities.

Movement of the Sun

Jenny and Jason made this drawing. What do you think about their ideas? You can change the drawing or the writing if you want to.

The Sun is a long way above the ground. It is bright and hot.

The Sun disappears and changes into the moon. Everywhere is dark.

How We See

Peri and Stevie made this drawing. What do you think about their ideas? You can change the drawing or the writing if you want to.

The light shines on the book.
I look at the book and see
the book because the light
is shining on it.

Games

What are games?

A game is an activity with an element of competition to provide a purpose for engaging with the game. Games may involve the use of dice, counters, boards, cards, models and so on. Usually they will involve some kind of counting, collecting or matching. They may involve a scoring system, a race to see who finishes first or a whole group collective activity with a common purpose. Science-related games can be built around common everyday games such as bingo, beetle drive and snakes and ladders.

How can you use games?

Games can be used at the start of or part way through a topic to provide a setting in which learners find out about some aspect of science. For example, a game in which learners have to throw dice to collect parts of a plant to make a complete plant can help them to learn the names of the stem, petals, roots and so on. Games can also be used for review purposes towards the end of an activity or topic. For example, there are numerous loop games available commercially which use cards with words on one half and definitions on the other half. Someone puts down a card, then another player has to match the word on the second half with a definition on one of their cards. This continues until all the cards are used and the cards form a complete loop.

Games are normally used as a group rather than an individual activity. However, within the group, learners may play as individuals or as part of a team, depending on the game. If they play as teams then games are a stimulus for discussion as they share their ideas and have to reach consensus within the team.

> **Whether learners are playing as individuals or as teams, games can be a challenge to their thinking.**

How can games help with assessment?

Games can give you access to the learners' ideas so that you can make assessment judgements, particularly if they are playing the game as individuals. It will be evident where they get confused or stuck, where they can't complete their turn or where they need to ask for help. By contrast, where the game runs smoothly it can help to confirm a judgement that the learners are fairly secure in that area.

How can games help with learning?

Whether learners are playing as individuals or as teams, games can be a challenge to their thinking. Games can provide an opportunity for learners to review their learning, clarify their thinking and consolidate their ideas. They can be useful for review and revision purposes as a light-hearted way of revisiting learning at the end of a lesson or topic. They are especially useful for motivating learners in areas of science where there is a lot of information to be dealt with (such as names, tables and definitions). They also provide opportunities for visual, auditory and kinaesthetic involvement which supports the different learning styles of individuals.

Examples of suitable topics for Snakes and Ladders could be: reactive (ladders) or unreactive (snakes) elements; positive (ladders) or negative factors (snakes) in energy efficiency; good (ladders) or poor (snakes) electrical or thermal conductors. Resources to play the games are on the CD. The skeleton game is adapted from Fawcett, M (1998).

68

The Skeleton Game

This is a collecting game using dice where you have to collect a complete skeleton. You need a card with the outline of the skeleton drawn in, or skeleton parts on cards.

Each of the parts of the skeleton has a different value.

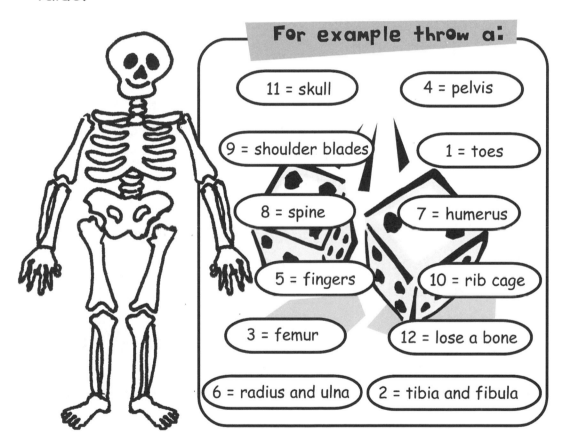

For example throw a:

- 11 = skull
- 4 = pelvis
- 9 = shoulder blades
- 1 = toes
- 8 = spine
- 7 = humerus
- 5 = fingers
- 10 = rib cage
- 3 = femur
- 12 = lose a bone
- 6 = radius and ulna
- 2 = tibia and fibula

Each player takes turns to throw the dice and collect parts or colour in the skeleton until you have a complete skeleton.

Snakes and Ladders

100	99	98	97	96	95	94	93	92	91
81									90
80									71
61									70
60									51
41									50
40									31
21									30
20									11
1	2	3	4	5	6	7	8	9	10

Create a dice game based on snakes and ladders. Each group needs a blank photocopied snakes and ladders board.

The boards have a range of different sizes of snakes and ladders. You need to decide on suitable descriptions for each of the snakes and ladders to complete the board before you can play the game. You can check these descriptions with your teacher before adding them to the board.

Graphic organisers:
compare and contrast

What is a compare and contrast graphic organiser?

Graphic organisers use some kind of visual framework to guide the learner's thinking. They may use a combination of text, diagrams, arrows, boxes, and so on. A compare and contrast graphic organiser uses a framework which invites learners to identify similarities and differences between two or more objects or events.

How can you use compare and contrast graphic organisers?

Compare and contrast graphic organisers can be used at the start of a topic to clarify the learners' initial ideas. They can be used partway through or at the end of a topic to review what has been learnt or to apply the new ideas that have been learnt. They are likely to be most useful where there is some kind of relationship between the things being compared. Examples of this could be where things look similar but are different in other ways (e.g. shark and dolphin); where processes lead to a similar outcome (e.g. boiling and evaporation); or where things are different but closely related (e.g. solids, liquids and gases).

Compare and contrast graphic organisers can be used as an individual or a small group activity. As an individual activity it can give you access to the learners' individual ideas. As a group activity it provides useful opportunities for discussion and scientific argument as they share their ideas within the group.

71

How can compare and contrast graphic organisers help with assessment?

The compare and contrast graphic organisers provide direct evidence of the learners' understanding, including their ability to apply ideas in a new situation. You can use these for assessment by reviewing the graphic organisers that the learners produce and making a judgement about the accuracy and completeness of their ideas. Potential misconceptions can be included in the graphic organiser framework. The completed graphic organisers can be scrutinised and assessment judgements made outside lesson time.

How can compare and contrast graphic organisers help with learning?

The purpose of the visual framework is to provide additional support for thinking and learning. The compare and contrast framework helps learners to review their learning and to make connections and identify relationships that may not be immediately obvious. It helps them to create the 'big picture' that enables them to make more sense of smaller details.

At a more general level graphic organisers provide opportunities for different types of thinking and for learners with different learning styles. The explicit framework for thinking helps them to become more aware of their own thinking processes (metacognition) and to begin to manage their own thinking.

Graphic organisers are adapted from Critical Thinking Books and Software: www.criticalthinking.com

Bird and Bat

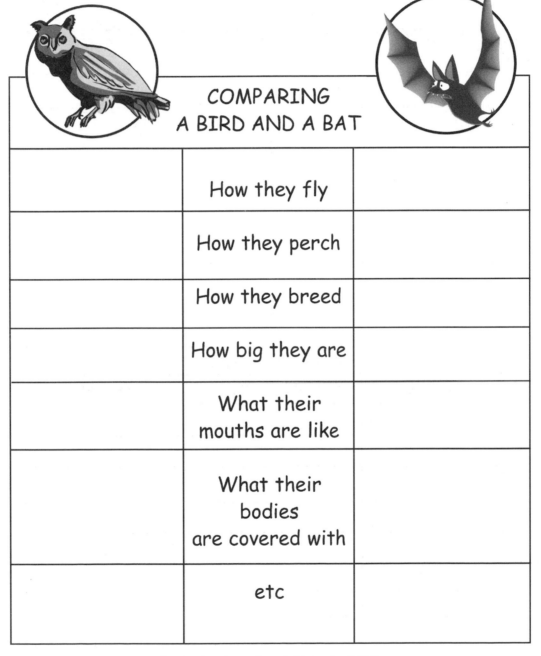

	COMPARING A BIRD AND A BAT	
	How they fly	
	How they perch	
	How they breed	
	How big they are	
	What their mouths are like	
	What their bodies are covered with	
	etc	

Photosynthesis

COMPARING PHOTOSYNTHESIS AND RESPIRATION

Main similarities
1.
2.
3.

Main differences		
Photosynthesis	in relation to . . .	Respiration

Graphic organisers:
reasoning by analogy

What is a reasoning by analogy graphic organiser?

Graphic organisers use some kind of visual framework to guide the learner's thinking. They may use a combination of text, diagrams, arrows, boxes, and so on. A reasoning by analogy graphic organiser uses a framework which invites learners to identify similarities between objects or events, such as structural or functional similarities.

How can you use reasoning by analogy graphic organisers?

Reasoning by analogy graphic organisers are likely to be used part way through or at the end of a topic to review what has been learnt or to apply the new ideas that have been learnt. They are used to illustrate some kind of relationship between the things being compared. This is likely to be a structural relationship (e.g. a tray of marbles being shaken and molecular movement in a liquid) or a functional relationship (e.g. the way that a flamingo's beak and a sieve work), though other kinds of relationship are also possible.

Reasoning by analogy graphic organisers can be used as an individual or a small group activity. As an individual activity it can give you access to the learners' individual ideas. As a group activity it provides a basis for debate and discussion as they share their ideas within the group.

75

How can reasoning by analogy graphic organisers help with assessment?

The reasoning by analogy graphic organisers provide evidence of the learners' understanding, including their ability to apply ideas in a new situation. You can use these for assessment by reviewing the graphic organisers that the learners produce and making a judgement about the accuracy and completeness of their ideas. Potential misconceptions can be included in the graphic organiser framework. The completed graphic organisers can be scrutinised and assessment judgements made outside lesson time.

How can reasoning by analogy graphic organisers help with learning?

The purpose of the visual framework is to provide additional support for thinking and learning. The reasoning by analogy framework helps learners to make connections between ideas, and to use models and analogies to help them understand more about a situation.

At a more general level graphic organisers provide opportunities for different types of thinking and for learners with different learning styles. The explicit framework for thinking helps them to become more aware of their own thinking processes (metacognition) and to begin to manage their own thinking.

Graphic organisers are adapted from Critical Thinking Books and Software: www.criticalthinking.com

Whale & Submarine

A WHALE IS LIKE A SUBMARINE BECAUSE:

1.

2.

3.

Electric Circuit

AN ELECTRIC CIRCUIT IS LIKE A CENTRAL HEATING SYSTEM BECAUSE . . .		
In an electric circuit ...		In a central heating system...
	Something flows around the system	Water flows in pipes between the boiler and the radiators
	The stuff flowing around the system doesn't get used up	
	Energy is transferred	
Energy is transferred from the battery to the lamp	You can have series or parallel arrangements	
Understanding how the central heating system works helps me to understand more about electric circuits because . . .		

78

Graphic organisers:
whole-parts relationships

What is a whole-parts relationship graphic organiser?

Graphic organisers use some kind of visual framework to guide the learner's thinking. They may use a combination of text, diagrams, arrows, boxes, and so on. A whole-parts relationship graphic organiser uses a framework which invites learners to identify functional and systemic relationships between objects or systems.

How can you use whole-parts relationship graphic organisers?

Whole-parts relationship graphic organisers are likely to be used part way through or at the end of a topic to review what has been learnt or to apply the new ideas that have been learnt. They are used to illustrate the nature of the relationship between the things being considered. By breaking down the relationship into sub-units the functions of the sub-units and the connections between them become more obvious. For example, the parts of a plant all work together to enable the plant to survive; the parts of an electric circuit work together to enable things to happen as a result of the flow of electricity; the organisms linked through feeding relationships in an ecosystem enable the system to remain relatively stable.

Whole-parts relationship graphic organisers can be used as an individual or a small group activity. As an individual activity it can give you access to the learners' individual ideas. As a group activity it provides a basis for debate and discussion as they share their ideas within the group.

79

How can whole-parts relationship graphic organisers help with assessment?

The whole-parts relationship graphic organisers provide evidence of the learners' understanding, including their ability to apply ideas in a new situation. You can provide partly-completed frameworks for learners to complete or get them to summarise the relationships between the parts. You can use these for assessment by reviewing the graphic organisers that the learners produce and making a judgement about the accuracy and completeness of their ideas. The completed graphic organisers can be scrutinised outside lesson time.

How can whole-parts relationship graphic organisers help with learning?

The purpose of the visual framework is to provide additional support for thinking and learning. The whole-parts relationship framework helps learners to make connections and identify functional relationships that may not be immediately obvious. It helps them to recognise the relevance of smaller details which enables them to make more sense of the 'big picture'.

At a more general level graphic organisers provide opportunities for different types of thinking and for learners with different learning styles. The explicit framework for thinking helps them to become more aware of their own thinking processes (metacognition) and to begin to manage their own thinking.

Graphic organisers are adapted from Critical Thinking Books and Software: www.criticalthinking.com

Eagle

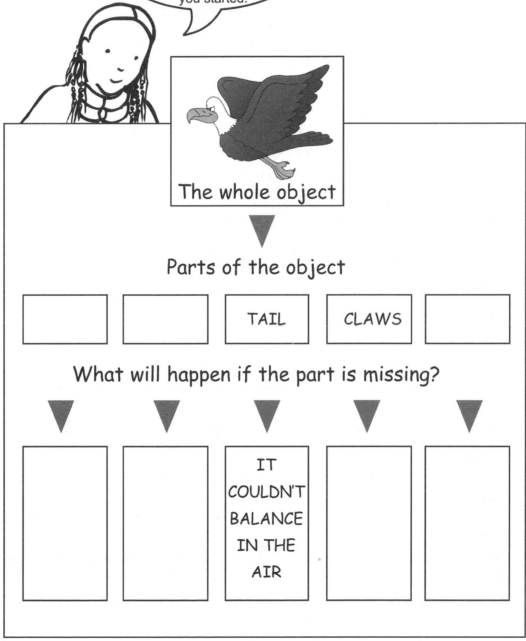

Can you complete the diagram below? Some of the boxes have been filled in to get you started.

The whole object

▼

Parts of the object

		TAIL	CLAWS	

What will happen if the part is missing?

▼ ▼ ▼ ▼ ▼

		IT COULDN'T BALANCE IN THE AIR		

81

Circulatory System

Can you complete the table below? Use the information to describe the relationship between...

the parts and the whole system.

THE WHOLE SYSTEM		
The circulatory system		
Parts of the system	What would happen to the system if this part were missing?	What is the function of this part of the system?
Heart	Blood would not circulate round the body	
Arteries		
Veins		Carry blood back to the heart
Capillaries		
Blood		
Valves		
Lymph vessels		
etc		

© S Naylor, B Keogh, A Goldsworthy (2004)

82

Generating a set
of instructions

What is generating a set of instructions?

Learners can generate a set of instructions that another person could follow.
The instructions set out what someone else has to do to achieve a particular
outcome.

How can you use generating a set of instructions?

Generating a set of instructions is likely to be used at the end of a topic as a way
of getting learners to review what they have learnt and to apply their learning. It
is in effect a form of recording, usually written, which sets out what they have
learnt. Usually it will apply to some kind of practical investigation. For example,
if you have been doing some work on germination then learners could generate a
set of instructions for how to get seeds to grow well, taking account of the
various factors that they have investigated.

It can be helpful to provide an everyday context for the instructions, in order to
create a sense of purpose for the activity. For example, the context for
instructions for getting seeds to grow well could be a Spring Fair at the school
where the learners have decided to buy seeds in bulk and sell them to parents in
smaller packets to make money for the school. Parents would need instructions
on the packets so that they know what to do with the seeds that they buy.

The approach can be used as an individual or as a small group activity. It may be
helpful to provide a writing frame to support this, depending on how complex
the instructions are and how fluent at writing the learners are (see the second
example). Alternatively support could be provided through a set of questions to
answer when producing the instructions (see the first example).

How can generating a set of instructions help with assessment?

Generating a set of instructions provides evidence of the learners' understanding which you can use to make assessment judgements, based on the accuracy, coherence and completeness of the instructions. For example, a set of instructions for an electrical circuit with three lamps which are all bright would show whether the learner understood the nature of a parallel circuit. As an individual activity it will provide evidence of each individual's understanding, though this loses the opportunity for discussion and scientific argument in groups.

How can generating a set of instructions help with learning?

Producing a set of instructions requires learners to review and clarify what they have learnt and to summarise their learning in a simple format. This is a useful way of consolidating their learning and highlighting any areas of uncertainty. Some opportunity to follow up any areas of uncertainty that are revealed will be helpful and will ensure that assessment is purposeful. Generating a set of instructions helps to prevent recording in science becoming too much of a routine and repetitive activity. As a group activity it will stimulate discussion and scientific argument as well as individual reflection on learning.

The first activity is based on an idea by Feasey, 1999: 67, where a set of instructions written by 9-year-olds can be seen.

Growing Seeds

Create a seed packet with a set of instructions to help someone to grow the seeds. The following questions should help you.

GROW YOUR OWN

1. What equipment will you need?
2. How much compost or soil do you put in the plant pot?
3. How deep do you plant the seed?
4. Which way up does the seed go?
5. How much water do you give it?
6. Where should you leave it - in the light or in the dark?
7. How warm does it have to be?

© S Naylor, B Keogh, A Goldsworthy (2004)

Rock Salt

Complete the following set of instructions.

HOW TO GET TABLE SALT FROM ROCK SALT

1   First grind the . . .

2   Then stir . . .

3   Next fold a . . .

4   Then filter the liquid to . . .

5   When you have done this, heat . . .

6   Then leave the beaker . . .

7   After a while you will get . . .

8   Collect the . . .   and dry them . . .

9   You can put the salt crystals on . . .

© S Naylor, B Keogh, A Goldsworthy (2004)

86

KWL grids

What are KWL grids?

KWL grids are simple 3-column grids which set out what learners think they **Know** about a topic, **Want** to know about the topic and have **Learnt** about the topic. Usually the number of entries are limited by the teacher depending on the age and experience of the learners.

How can you use KWL grids?

KWL grids will be used both at the start of a topic to identify what learners already know and at the end of the topic to review what they have learnt. The first stage in the grid could form a useful homework exercise, either by learners writing their ideas in the grid at home or by thinking about what they already know so that they can share their ideas in the next lesson. The grids can be provided as a handout for learners to complete the first two sections individually. Alternatively they can be used by small groups who pool their ideas and the questions that they want to research. This gives less information about their individual ideas but can be a more creative process. It also can help to support less fluent writers.

Another approach is to complete the first section individually or in small groups and then to use this as the basis for a class discussion in which all the ideas and questions are pooled. This gives you an opportunity to manage the discussion and to maximise the connections with your existing scheme of work. It also allows you to emphasise the wide variety of ways of finding out that are available and to identify which of the questions lend themselves to practical investigation. However, it is important that learners have some degree of control over which questions they pursue, otherwise they will see little purpose in using the grids.

How can KWL grids help with assessment?

The grids are useful for assessment in that they give direct access to what learners feel they know at the start of the topic and to what they believe they have learnt at the end. Usually the grids will be in written form, but they can also be recorded in other ways, such as an adult scribing ideas for non-fluent writers or by using a tape recorder.

How can KWL grids help with learning?

KWL grids provide a structure for learners to organise their thinking and help to make the connection between prior knowledge and future learning. At the start of a topic the focus is on what learners already know. The grid helps them to clarify their existing knowledge and to identify the boundaries of their understanding. The second section sets out how their learning can build on what they already know. The grid prompts them into setting relevant questions, emphasises their role as learners and helps them to play an active role in modifying and developing their ideas. The final section identifies what learning has occurred. It helps learners to review and consolidate their learning and enables them to see the positive outcomes of their research.

You can use the examples to illustrate the use of KWL grids and to generate discussion about the ideas. There is a blank grid provided on the CD.

Teeth

Do you agree with the ideas that Ranju has written in the first column? You can change any that you do not agree with.

Add three more ideas and three things that you would like to find out about.

RANJU'S KWL GRID

3 things I THINK I KNOW already about teeth	3 things I WANT to know about teeth	What I have LEARNT about teeth
They fall out every year and new ones grow	Why do they fall out?	
I need to brush them	What happens if I don't brush my teeth?	
The dentist looks after them	What things are good for my teeth?	

89

Light

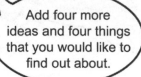

Do you agree with the ideas that Nikki has written in the first column? You can change any that you do not agree with.

Add four more ideas and four things that you would like to find out about.

NIKKI'S KWL GRID

5 things I THINK I KNOW already about light	5 things I WANT to know about light	What I have LEARNT about light
We get light from the sun, the moon and electric lights	Where does darkness come from?	
You can mix light to make new colours like you can with paint	How do you get rainbows?	
A shadow is a reflection of a person on the ground	Can you get coloured shadows?	
It goes dark really quickly when you turn off the light	How far away can you see a torch?	

Writing a letter

What is writing a letter?

Writing a letter is an alternative way of recording scientific ideas. It is a means of creating a purpose and a context for learners to put down their ideas in print. The letter can be to a person (real or imaginary), a character or an organisation.

How can you use writing a letter?

You can use writing a letter to get learners to raise a problem (e.g. inefficient use of energy by an organisation), to describe an idea (e.g. how to make something float really well) or to outline the results of an investigation (e.g. which materials are waterproof). Writing a letter is probably most useful at the end of an activity or topic as a written summary of what has been learnt. Although letters can be suitable at an earlier stage in an activity, they are unlikely to provide as much assessment evidence as when they are used at the end.

Writing a letter can be used as an individual or a small group activity. As an individual activity it can give you access to the learners' individual ideas. As a group activity it provides a basis for debate and discussion as they share their ideas within the group. With younger learners it may be helpful to provide support for the writing process, for example by scribing for them, using a simple writing frame, producing a word bank or providing sentence stems.

How can writing a letter help with assessment?

Writing a letter can be used to make assessment judgements about the learners' ideas based on the accuracy, coherence and completeness of the contents of the letters. The letters provide evidence of learning, such as what conclusions have been drawn from an investigation. They provide a permanent record of the learners' ideas which you can look at outside lesson time if necessary.

How can writing a letter help with learning?

The most important aspect of writing a letter is that it offers a motivating stimulus for writing. Sometimes writing about science can be demotivating because it is viewed as routine and purposeless. Writing a letter to a named person or organisation makes the writing more enjoyable because the purpose is clear and there is scope for individuality and creativity. It also provides an opportunity for learners to review their learning, clarify their thinking and consolidate their ideas.

If learners take their letter writing seriously then they will probably hope to get a reply. This can be a useful lead-in to further learning, since the replies may raise questions which the learners need to investigate. When the letters are to an imaginary character or person then you (or older learners in the school) can write the reply. This gives you an opportunity to include deliberately in the reply some of the questions which could be used as a stimulus for the next activity or topic. Younger learners may need support in writing a letter, such as the one to Fred Bear. However, during this process they will be sharing and reviewing their ideas.

Fred Bear's Coat

Now, where did I leave my raincoat?

Fred Bear has a problem. He has managed to lose his raincoat. You need to find out which fabric or material would be best to make him a new one. You can then write to him to say what you have found out.

Your letter is likely to include:

◤ What you have done to help Fred.

◤ How you tested the different fabrics and materials.

◤ What you found out from the tests.

◤ Which fabric would be best for Fred's coat and why.

Disposable Cup

THE PROBLEM

THE DISPOSABLE CUPS USED FOR TAKE-OUT DRINKS FROM THE LOCAL FAST FOOD OUTLET ARE TOO HOT TO PICK UP EASILY AND THEY ARE NOT BIODEGRADABLE. YOU NEED TO INVESTIGATE WHICH MATERIALS ARE BIODEGRADABLE AND WHAT INEXPENSIVE METHODS COULD BE USED FOR THERMALLY INSULATING THE CUP. YOU WILL THEN NEED TO WRITE A LETTER TO THE FAST FOOD OUTLET TELLING THEM WHAT YOU HAVE FOUND OUT.

Your letter is likely to include:

◣ Why there is a problem with the cups currently used.

◣ What the outlet could use instead of their normal cups.

◣ How this would help to solve the problem.

◣ Whether there might be any additional consequences of changing the cups.

◣ What might be the consequence of not changing from the cups currently used.

Making a list

What is making a list?

When learners make a list they use a simple framework in list format to capture what they know about a topic. This could include a list of events, processes, ideas, connections, objects or parts of an object.

How can you use making a list?

Making a list can be used at the start of a topic as a stimulus for getting learners to reflect on what they already know about that topic or to generate ideas and possibilities. For example, they can list what they think are the factors that might affect the germination of seeds and this could then be used as the basis for designing an investigation. Making a list can be used part way through or at the end of a topic as a way of getting learners to review what they have learnt and to apply their learning. For example, they can list all the words that are associated with a change of state (evaporating, freezing, solidifying, etc) and the definitions that go with them.

The approach can be used as an individual or as a small group activity. It can be a class-based or a homework activity in preparation for an investigation, or it might be part of a whole-class conclusion to an investigation or enquiry. It may be helpful to provide a writing frame to support this, depending on how complex the list is and how fluent at writing the learners are.

How can making a list help with assessment?

Making a list provides evidence of the learners' ideas which you can use to make assessment judgements, based on the wording used and the accuracy and completeness of the list. The simple framework used can make it easy to identify potential uncertainties and misconceptions. As an individual activity it will provide evidence of each individual's ideas, though the advantage of using this as a group activity is that it will stimulate discussion and scientific argument as well as individual reflection.

How can making a list help with learning?

Making a list can help with learning in a variety of ways, depending on the type of list and how it is used. A list of possibilities can be a stimulus to creative thinking; a list of processes can help to make connections between concepts; a list of differences between processes can help to understand relationships; a list of definitions can help to consolidate learning. Resolving differences of opinion through argument and the use of evidence when this is a group activity is another important aspect of learning.

A 'pull' list is on the CD to use with the 'push' list activity.

Push and Pull Walk

Go on a 'push-pull' walk around the school. You are in the push team. As you walk round look for pushes. How many pushes can you find for your team? We have given you some ideas to start with. We will compare our ideas with the pull team when we get back to the classroom.

THE PUSH TEAM	
WE SAW THESE PUSHES	A PICTURE OF THE PUSH
Teacher opening the door	
Caretaker opening the window	
The cook moving the trolley out of the way	

97

Light and Sound

WHAT I KNOW ABOUT LIGHT AND SOUND

CHARACTERISTICS	LIGHT	SOUND
What are the sources?		
How does it travel?		
How fast does it travel?		
How is it reflected?		
How is it refracted?		

Matching exercises

What are matching exercises?

In a matching exercise learners make connections between two sets of information. Typically one set of information is a list of names and the other set is a list of descriptions or definitions, though there are other possible information sets that can be matched together.

How can you use matching exercises?

Matching exercises can be used at the start of a topic to check what learners already know or to review previous learning in an earlier topic. For example, a quick review of the main parts of a skeleton could be a useful lead-in to more detailed work on a particular aspect of the skeletal system. Matching exercises are more commonly used part way through or at the end of a topic to review and consolidate the learning. For example, at the end of a topic on changes of state a matching exercise could be used to review the meanings of the various definitions, such as freezing, boiling, evaporating and so on.

Matching exercises require a bit of advance preparation in deciding on the sets of information to present and a suitable means of presenting them. For example, you might have a set of pictures down one side of a page and a set of words down the other side, so that learners have to draw lines to match the pictures and words (parts of a flower, for example). You might have a set of names or definitions on cards (such as elements, compounds, molecules) which learners have to match with a set of examples (such as water, air, nitrogen, bread and so on). You might have a series of powerpoint slides with a set of bulleted descriptions of types of rock which learners have to match with the name of the type of rock .

Matching exercises can be a group or an individual activity. As a group activity they will provide a useful stimulus for discussion as learners share their ideas and try to reach consensus within the group. They can also be used for homework, either as a lead-in to the following lesson or as a review of recent learning.

How can matching exercises help with assessment?

Matching exercises provide access to the learners' ideas so that you can make assessment judgements based on the accuracy and completeness of the match. The simple framework used can make it easy to identify potential uncertainties and misconceptions. This can enable you to decide whether any further work or additional support is needed in this area.

How can matching exercises help with learning?

Matching exercises are helpful for summarising, reviewing and consolidating learning. They can help learners to put together information which may have been learnt in fragments over a period of time so that the bigger picture is clarified and reinforced. They can also have a role in revision after a topic has finished, where information learnt previously is represented in a different format in order to consolidate learning.

There are cards for a rock bingo game on the CD.

Flower Parts

Can you match the parts of a flower with the descriptions of what the parts do?

Draw a line from the name to the description.

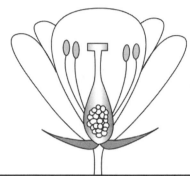

NAME OF THE PART	WHAT THE PART DOES
Stamen	This is the female part of the flower. It produces the egg cells that turn into seeds when they are fertilised.
Stigma	This is the outer part which protects the flower as it is developing. It is usually green.
Petal	This is the male part of the flower. It produces the pollen.
Pollen	This is usually brightly coloured and scented to attract insects.
Ovary	This is the part that catches the pollen. It is usually sticky so that the pollen doesn't fall off easily.
Sepal	This is the part that gets carried to another flower to fertilise it.

Rock Bingo

Match the descriptions with names of rocks. You can do this as a bingo game by either choosing 6 of the rocks each or by using bingo cards. One person will need to read out the descriptions at random.

DESCRIPTIONS

A metamorphic rock formed from sandstone

A sedimentary rock formed from shells

An igneous rock which cools slowly underground

A metamorphic rock formed from mudstone

A rock formed from other rocks by high pressure and temperature

An igneous rock with small crystals or a glassy structure

A metamorphic rock formed from limestone

BINGO

	SLATE	LIME-STONE		GRANITE
SAND-STONE			QUARTZ	BASALT

News reports

What are news reports?

In a news report learners present information in the style of a media report of an interesting or a hypothetical event.

How can you use news reports?

The news reports could be entirely text-based, such as a newspaper report; they could involve more than one format, such as text, graphics and pictures in a news magazine; they could use electronic media, such as in a radio or TV report or a web page; they could be multi-media, such as a powerpoint presentation involving text, pictures, graphics, video clips and/or internet links.

News reports are most likely to be used part way through or at the end of a topic. They can be a group or an individual activity, and they can be used in class or for homework. They can be planned jointly as a class activity and then finished individually for homework. The benefits of producing a collaborative news report are that ideas can be shared, challenged and developed jointly.

The important aspect of news reports is that they provide an opportunity for creativity in science, especially creative writing. For example, at the end of a topic on forces learners could produce a news report on friction, as though it is a force that has just been discovered. Similarly, part way through a topic on plant reproduction learners could produce a news report on how plant male reproductive cells manage to make their way to female reproductive cells, stressing how inventive plants have been in evolutionary terms (or possibly stressing the parallels with human teenage behaviour). They can be produced for ordinary everyday events in science lessons, but presented in a creative way.

103

> **News reports are a good example of how learning in science can be linked with learning in literacy.**

A news report containing deliberate mistakes can also be used as the starting point for an activity. Learners can check the accuracy of the report in a follow up activity. The report acts as a writing frame to support learners in producing their own report.

How can news reports help with assessment?

News reports can be used for assessment in that they provide direct access to the learners' ideas, either individually or in groups. This allows you to make judgements about how creative they have been, their level of understanding and any possible uncertainties or misconceptions. You can then decide whether any further work or additional support is needed in this area.

How can news reports help with learning?

As with any group activity, discussion of what to put in a news report helps to clarify the learners' ideas and invites them to consider what evidence is available to support their ideas. It can help learners to identify their own uncertainties and to want to find out more. Being expected to think creatively helps learners to review and rethink what they already know and consolidate their learning. It also motivates them to engage with the activity and prevents recording in science becoming too much of a routine procedure. News reports are a good example of how learning in science can be linked with learning in literacy.

The examples can be used as illustrations or to generate discussion about the accuracy of the report or the issues involved.

Vanishing Sugar

The DAILY NEWS

45P

SUGAR DISAPPEARS AS YOU WATCH!

Children in the Year 5 class at Elm Street School made a surprising discovery yesterday. They had been mixing substances such as sand and flour with water. When they tried this with sugar they were amazed when the sugar seemed to disappear.

"We just put it in the water and watched and watched and eventually the sugar disappeared", said Ben, a pupil in Mrs Bianchi's class. Other pupils in the class had

Exclusive by
Miss Knowbody

CASTER disappears without trace. Last seen jumping into a jug of water.

seen the same thing happening. "I think it went slower when we stirred it", said Shanaz. Her friend Gina also thought that it disappeared faster

when they used cold water.

Mrs Bianchi plans to try this with lots more substances in her science lessons. Her assistant investigators are busy making lists of substances that they predict will disappear. They hope to see some more disappearing acts soon!

A local scientist was asked for her comments. She said that she was surprised by the children's results.

What do you think about the report?

Why not try out your ideas and write a report for the newspaper.

Cosmic Storm

A RADIO REPORT ON THE 6 O'CLOCK NEWS

Do you think this could ever happen?
Write a radio report about your ideas.

Odd one out

What is odd one out?

An odd one out activity involves learners selecting the odd one out from a list of objects or events and justifying their reasoning. It could be an insulator from a group of conductors, a metal from a group of non-metals, a reversible change from a list of permanent changes, a plant from a group of fixed animals such as barnacles, and so on.

How can you use odd one out?

The odd one out approach can be used at the start of a topic as a stimulus for getting learners to reflect on what they already know about that topic. It will help them to think about what possible groupings there could be, what the criteria are for separating the objects or events into different groups and how the criteria apply to the list. It can be used part way through or at the end of a topic as a way of getting learners to apply their ideas and make connections between different bits of information.

The approach can be used as an individual or as a small group activity. It can be a class-based or a homework activity in preparation for some kind of follow-up investigation, or it might be used as a whole-class conclusion to an investigation or enquiry. The advantage of using this as a group activity is that it will stimulate discussion and scientific argument as well as individual reflection.

The approach lends itself to producing a list on a handout, display or overhead transparency. Pictures as well as words can be used, especially with younger learners or those that are not yet fluent readers.

Learners can be asked to produce their own odd one out lists. This can be a challenging activity, similar to Generating questions (page 119).

How can odd one out help with assessment?

You can use this approach for assessment by checking which items are picked as the odd ones out and the reasoning behind the choices. Often the reasoning will be more important than the actual choice since it gives you more complete access to the learners' ideas. If they are in written format then you can scrutinise them and make assessment judgements after the lesson if necessary.

How can odd one out help with learning?

Deciding which is the odd one out involves learners in making judgements. They need to compare and contrast, to look for evidence (e.g. whether evaporation is a reversible change) and to apply their ideas. Critical thinking will be involved, and learners will generally want to go on to carry out a further investigation or enquiry to help confirm their judgements.

As the learners discuss their ideas they may well change their ideas. Justifying their own ideas, listening to the other learners' views and discussing what evidence is available forms an important part of their learning.

Light Sources

WHICH IS THE ODD ONE OUT
IN THE FOLLOWING AND WHY?

1

White lines in the road
A car headlight
A bike reflector
'Cat's eyes' in the road

WHY?

2

A piece of white paper
A picture
A television
A mirror

WHY?

3

A Christmas tree decoration
Aluminium foil
A traffic warden's coat
A torch

WHY?

4

The Sun
The Moon
The Earth
The planet Venus

WHY?

5

A knife
A belt buckle
A burning candle
A drawing pin

WHY?

Changes

WHICH IS THE ODD ONE OUT IN THE FOLLOWING AND WHY?

1 Stretching. Bending. Rusting. | WHY?

2 Grinding. Dissolving. Distilling. | WHY?

3 Burning. Melting. Evaporating. | WHY?

4 Dissolving. Neutralising. Filtering. | WHY?

5 Corroding. Scraping. Painting. | WHY?

6 Mixing. Beating. Baking. | WHY?

7 Fermenting. Condensing. Freezing. | WHY?

Posters

What are posters?

A poster is usually a large-scale annotated drawing in which learners express their ideas. They are commonly used to describe processes and relationships which are difficult to describe in words. The balance between the amount of drawing and text in the poster can vary.

How can you use posters?

Posters can be used at the start of a topic to get learners to share their understanding of how they think certain events occur, such as day and night or convection currents in fluids. The posters then help to identify areas of uncertainty and create an agenda for learning more about those areas.

They can be used part way through or at the end of a topic, to show what the learners think is happening or how they think something is happening. This can be a useful way to review learning and make links between different aspects of learning. For example, they could be used to get learners to summarise how different organisms in a habitat are connected or how particle theory helps them to make sense of changes of state.

Although posters can be produced by individuals this is generally a small group activity. It provides a basis for debate and discussion as they share their ideas within the group.

How can posters help with assessment?

The poster can be used for assessment since it gives you direct access to learners' ideas in the way that they choose to represent them. It does not usually give detailed information about individual ideas. However, producing the poster is a collaborative activity so the finished poster normally represents a consensus of ideas within the group. Individuals could be asked to summarise the key ideas on the poster as if presenting an advertising campaign to a client. As a semi-permanent record, posters can be scrutinised outside lesson time when you can look for evidence of good understanding, uncertainty or misconceptions.

How can posters help with learning?

Personalising their ideas in a poster is usually a motivating stimulus for learners. As with any group activity, discussion of what to put in the poster helps to clarify their ideas, invites them to consider what evidence is available to support their ideas and creates a sense of purpose for follow up activities. Producing a poster can help learners to identify their own uncertainties and so generate the need to find out more. At the end of a topic, posters are particularly useful for helping learners to make connections and to begin to build up the 'big pictures' of science.

The following can be used as illustrations of posters. There is a poster framework on the CD.

Cats' Eyes

What do you think? Fill in the rest of the poster to share your ideas.

113

Light Bulb

What do you think? Fill in the rest of the poster to share your ideas.

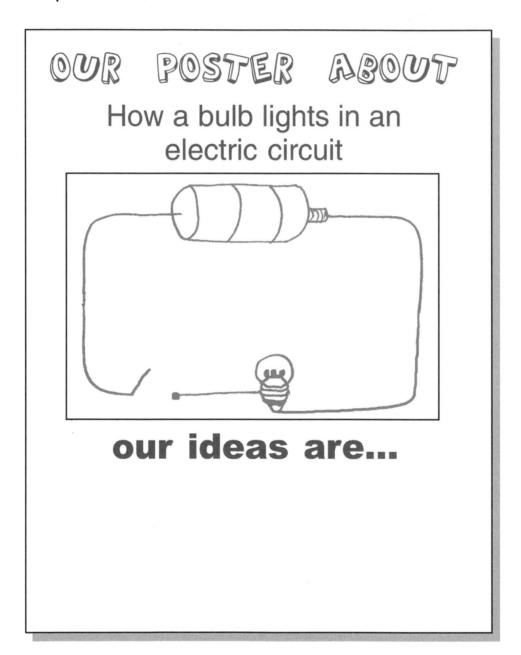

Predict, observe, explain

What is a predict, observe, explain sequence?

A predict, observe, explain sequence is one in which learners are expected to predict the outcome of an event, observe what actually happens, then explain why their prediction was either correct or incorrect.

How can you use predict, observe, explain?

Predict, observe, explain sequences are especially useful at the start of a topic as a way of getting learners thinking about the types of factors that are likely to be involved in a situation. They are also useful part way through a topic as a way of getting learners to apply their learning in a new situation. For example, they might be expected to predict whether a screwed up piece of paper will fall faster, slower or at the same speed as a flat piece of paper. This will involve them in reasoning about the relative effects of gravitational attraction and air resistance to make their prediction and explain what happens in practice.

The most engaging predict, observe, explain sequences are those which take learners by surprise or which seem to be counter-intuitive. Examples of counter-intuitive predict, observe, explain sequences are shown on the following page. White and Gunstone (1992: 44-56) also provide a range of creative examples of predict, observe, explain sequences.

It is important for learners to make a personal commitment to a prediction before making their observations. They can do the predict, observe, explain sequence as an individual activity, making their own prediction and then their observations. Alternatively, it can be a small group activity, with discussion

> " From the learner's point of
> view the prediction generates
> personal engagement with
> the ideas involved. "

about the situation followed by individuals in the group making a commitment to a specific prediction.

How can predict, observe, explain help with assessment?

This approach gives you access to the learners' ideas so you can use these as a basis for assessment. You can make assessment judgements about their initial predictions, why they make these predictions and how they explain what they actually observe. Explanations of discrepancies between their predictions and their observations are particularly useful for assessment.

How can predict, observe, explain help with learning?

From the teacher's point of view the initial prediction makes the learners' ideas explicit and helps to identify any misconceptions or misunderstandings. From the learner's point of view the prediction generates personal engagement with the ideas involved, so that the observation becomes a personally meaningful activity. The follow-up explanation offers a further opportunity for reflection, discussion and debate. It is likely that the predict, observe, explain sequence will generate the need for further investigation or research to clarify some of the questions that have arisen in the activity.

Floating and Sinking

Write your prediction. Watch what happens.
Try to explain what happens.

Electric Circuit

What do you think will happen to the lamp when the switch is closed?

Write your prediction.
Observe what happens.
Try to explain what happens.

Questions:
generating questions

What is generating questions?

The usual arrangement for questioning in classrooms is that the teacher asks the questions and the learners attempt to answer them. Generating questions puts the learners in a different role and gets them to think of questions that it would be useful to ask about a topic.

How can you use generating questions?

Generating questions can be used at any time. At the start of a topic they can be used to explore what learners already know and where their uncertainties lie (e.g. questions about the air). Part way through or at the end of a topic they can be used to help learners to reflect on and review their learning or to apply learning in a new setting. It is helpful to provide a suitable stimulus, such as a picture or a problem, around which learners can generate questions. This is especially important with younger learners. It can be useful to provide question stems on cards or a classroom display for them to use, such as "Why does . . ?" or "What if . . ?" or "How would . . ?", since these emphasise thinking rather than recall of information.

You can use generating questions with individual learners. However, they will probably not find it easy and they will probably not be very confident, so generating questions as a small group activity is more likely to be successful. It can be useful to model generating questions with a class ("Let's think up some good questions together about electricity") and to discuss why questions that require thinking (such as, "Do the cells die when an animal dies?") are more useful than questions that require only recall. The questions generated can be

> " Learners generally think that asking questions is easy and answering them is difficult. "

collated into a class display; one or more could be a focus for the next lesson; or learners could select one to think and write about for homework.

How can generating questions help with assessment?

You can use generating questions for assessment by making judgements about the number, quality and range of questions produced. Since this is an opportunity for creative thinking, creativity also ought to be noted and valued. Their questions will reveal what they understand and the limits of their understanding. If learners write down the questions which they generate then this provides a permanent record which you can scrutinise outside lesson time if you choose. White and Gunstone (1992) provide exceptionally good additional guidance on how you can use generating questions for assessment.

How can generating questions help with learning?

Learners generally think that asking questions is easy and answering them is difficult. They can get quite a shock when they have to produce their own questions, especially if the emphasis is on 'thinking questions' rather than recall questions. They realise very quickly that you have to understand a topic extremely well to be able to generate questions on that topic - which is why teachers can be so good at generating questions. In this way generating questions helps learners to recognise the level of their personal understanding and helps them to identify areas of personal uncertainty.

A list of question stems, which can be used to create other questions, is on the CD and on the poster which comes with this book.

Sound and Music

After a music lesson some children were invited to think of interesting questions about sounds. They used question words to help them think.

How does . . . . ?
How do . . . . . . ?
I wonder whether . . . . . . ?
How would we find. . . . . . ?
Do you think. . . . . . ?
What would. . . . . . ?
Would you expect. . . . . . ?
Why are. . . . . . ?
Where do. . . . . . ?

They came up with these questions:

- How does air make so many different sounds?

- I wonder whether big instruments always make loud sounds?

- How would we find out how far a sound can travel?

- Do you think that sounds can go round corners?

- Would you expect most musicians to go deaf?

- How do ear muffs protect your ears against sounds?

Use the same question words to think of your own questions.

Van Helmont

THE PICTURE SHOWS AN EXPERIMENT CARRIED OUT BY VAN HELMONT, A DUTCH SCIENTIST. HE WANTED TO FIND OUT WHERE THE EXTRA WEIGHT COMES FROM WHEN PLANTS GROW. WHAT QUESTIONS WOULD YOU LIKE TO ASK HIM ABOUT HIS EXPERIMENT IF HE VISITED US TODAY?

AFTER FIVE YEARS THE PLANT GAINS 164 POUNDS AND THE SOIL LOSES 2 OUNCES IN WEIGHT.

SOME USEFUL QUESTION STEMS ARE:

Why did . . . ?	Did you . . . ?	What if . . . ?
How did you . . . ?	How accurate. . ?	Could you have . . ?

HERE ARE SOME EXAMPLES:

- Did you weigh the water when you watered the plant?

- Did you keep the plant in the dark or in the light?

- What if some soil got blown away by the wind? Did you stop this happening?

- How did you get all the soil off the roots to weigh it after 5 years?

- Did you weigh the plant with leaves or without leaves?

Use the question stems to think of questions that you would like to ask Van Helmont.

Questions:
responding to questions

What is responding to questions?

The nature of responding to questions is very obvious: you ask a question and the learners attempt to answer it. Teachers tend to use questions constantly. However, the purpose of responding to questions, and how they might be used to support learning and assessment, is less obvious.

How can you use responding to questions?

Responding to questions can be used at any time. At the start of a topic they can be used to explore what learners already know and where their uncertainties lie. At the end of a topic they can be used to help learners to reflect on and review their learning or to apply their learning in a new setting. They can be used at any time to invite learners to think creatively and to solve problems.

The format for responding to questions can vary. You can use verbal, pictorial, written or electronic questions; you can use them as a class or a homework activity or as part of a display; they can involve an individual or a small group activity. The questions can be differentiated, targeted to individuals or open to everyone. The responses to the questions can be immediate or can form the focus for enquiry or discussion during a lesson; they can be oral or written; they can be produced by individuals or by groups.

How can responding to questions help with assessment?

You can use responding to questions for assessment because the learners' responses can provide a direct insight into their knowledge, understanding and

> **The most useful questions
> for learning are those
> which require more than
> just recall.**

thinking. Questions which require thinking, such as analysis, evaluation or inference, are generally more valuable for assessment than recall questions. Written responses to questions provide a permanent record which you can assess outside lesson time if you choose.

How can responding to questions help with learning?

The most useful questions for learning are those which require more than just recall and which get the learners thinking. Interesting or unusual questions which pose problems that the learners haven't thought about before are especially useful (such as, "Will there be any gravity in a room with no air?"). Open and person-centred questions (questions which start with, "What do you think . . ?") are generally most productive (see Harlen, 2000). So are questions which involve justifying their ideas, listening to other people's views and reaching a consensus based on the evidence available.

One of the problems with responding to questions in whole-class discussion and plenaries is that they may involve very few learners. They can be made more engaging by responding to questions with buddies or in groups; also by simple techniques such as not allowing any hands up, increasing the amount of thinking time before anyone answers, not evaluating their responses (e.g. "Does anybody have any other ideas?" rather than, "Yes, that's right") and involving the learners in evaluating the responses. Black et al (2002) provide very valuable guidance for how to manage questioning in the classroom.

The activities are designed to promote thinking beyond the recall of facts.

Light and Shadows

YOUR SHADOW KEEPS ON FOLLOWING YOU AROUND. HOW DO YOU THINK YOU CAN GET RID OF IT?

- Does your shadow have a face?
  Is it the same as your face?

- Which way up is your shadow?
  Does it have the head at the top and the feet at the bottom?

- What colour is your shadow?
  How do you think you can change its colour?

- Why do you think your shadow disappears at night?
  Where do you think it goes to?

What do you think?

© S Naylor, B Keogh, A Goldsworthy (2004)

125

Ready Steady Cook!

WHAT IS THE DIFFERENCE BETWEEN:

Boiling water and boiling an egg?

Pouring milk on your cornflakes and burning the toast?

Roasting coffee beans and making fresh coffee?

Whipping cream and making meringue?

Making ginger beer and making orange squash?

Making salad dressing and making a cake?

Caramelising sugar and melting lard?

Mixing water with wine and taking an indigestion tablet?

What do you think?

Sales pitch or advertisement

What are sales pitches or advertisements?

A sales pitch or advertisement is a way of presenting information to make a case for something. It can be to sell something, to get people to agree to something, to interest people in doing something, and so on. It is designed to interest people and capture their attention. It may present one side of a case rather than a balanced argument.

How can you use sales pitches or advertisements?

You can use sales pitches or advertisements as a way of getting the learners to research and present information in an interesting way. They lend themselves well to topics where there is a lot of information and you are faced with the question of how to offer learners access to information without simply 'lecturing' them. In these circumstances a research activity can be a more motivating way for learners to find out what they need to know. They are particularly useful in topics which involve building on what the learners already know, so that they need to review, rethink and develop their learning in this new context.

Learners can create sales pitches or advertisements individually. However, they are more valuable as a small group activity where ideas can be shared, challenged and developed collaboratively and the group interaction promotes engagement with the activity.

127

> ❝ **Creating a sales pitch or advertisement gives research-based activities a clear sense of purpose...** ❞

Sales pitches or advertisements are likely to include pictures as well as text. They could be multimedia (e.g. involving graphics, powerpoint presentations, or even video clips), depending on what skills the learners have and what time and resources are available. They can be short activities or extended over several days.

How can sales pitches or advertisements help with assessment?

The sales pitch or advertisement provides evidence of the learners' understanding. You can use them for assessment by marking them against specific criteria (e.g. accuracy of information presented, comprehensiveness, creativity and accessibility of the ideas for the particular audience) and making judgements about how much learning has occurred. If individual assessments are required then learners can be asked to produce a short slogan which summarises the key ideas in the advertisement.

How can sales pitches or advertisements help with learning?

Creating a sales pitch or advertisement gives research-based activities a clear sense of purpose and turns what can be a mechanical activity into one which is more personal and engaging. The sales pitch or advertisement helps to focus the learners' research, requires assimilation and reworking of the information and therefore helps to prevent them simply copying chunks of text out of a book or from internet sites. It also provides a purpose for reviewing existing learning and applying it in new circumstances.

Home for a frog is adapted from SATIS (1992).

Home for a Frog

CAN YOU MAKE AN ADVERTISEMENT FOR THEM?

You will need to think about questions like:

◤ What do frogs need to live?

◤ Where will they get their food?

◤ What kinds of things might damage or eat frogs?

◤ How will they be protected?

◤ Where will the tadpoles grow up?

129

Favourite Metal

YOU PLAN TO ENTER AN EXHIBITION FOR THE CREATIVE USE OF METALS. THERE IS A PRIZE FOR THE BEST EXHIBIT. YOU NEED TO CONVINCE THE SELECTION PANEL THAT YOUR CHOICE OF METAL IS THE BEST.

Choose your favourite metal and create an advertisement for it.

You will need to think about:

◤ What are its properties?

◤ What kinds of things could you use it for?

◤ How do its properties make it suitable?

◤ What makes it better than any other metals?

Use your imagination as well as your knowledge when you create your advertisement.

© S Naylor, B Keogh, A Goldsworthy (2004)

Sequencing:
statements, pictures and ideas

What is sequencing?

Sequencing involves taking a set of statements, pictures or ideas about a scientific process or processes and putting them into a logical order.

How can you use sequencing?

The format for the sequencing will depend on the age and maturity of the learners. Older learners might sequence abstract ideas or statements which are largely text-based, while younger learners are more likely to sequence concrete events which may be represented in pictures. Sequences can be temporary and dismantled at the end of a lesson. Alternatively, they may be semi-permanent, with a written outcome or a set of statements or cards stuck onto a piece of paper. For learners of any age, having something tangible to sequence, such as cards that can be physically rearranged, is always helpful. Learners can be presented with an incomplete sequence to complete. They can be produced individually or they can provide an opportunity for collaborative talking and thinking about the ideas in the sequence. The section on cartoon strip sequences (page 23) provides further ideas.

Sequencing could be used at the start of an enquiry to invite the learners to share their initial ideas or to make predictions about what they think will happen. For example, they might put the phases of the Moon into a sequence. Thinking about the sequence acts as an invitation to consider why the Moon appears to change shape and what is happening in the Earth-Moon system to cause these changes.

It is more likely that sequencing will be used towards the end of an enquiry as part of a review of their ideas. For example, they might sequence the stages in ecological succession in an ecosystem such as a sand dune. This might be part of an activity to model the various stages in succession after investigating a real life sand dune system.

How can sequencing help with assessment?

The sequences that the learners produce provide evidence of their understanding. You can use sequencing for assessment by reviewing the sequences that the learners generate and making a judgement about the accuracy of their ideas. It is generally more effective for sequences to be produced in groups, but individuals can create their own sequences which are then discussed in groups or which follow on from a group discussion.

How can sequencing help with learning?

As the learners discuss a possible sequence they will clarify their ideas, think about what evidence they have to support their ideas and identify areas of uncertainty. At the start of an enquiry this helps to create a sense of purpose for them in the follow up activity. It can help to focus their observations or research since they know what they want to learn about. It can also help the teacher to target certain aspects of the activity in response to the learners' ideas. Towards the end of an enquiry it can help them to review and consolidate their ideas as they apply their ideas in a new situation.

Change of State

The diagram below shows how water can change its state but some of the words are missing.

Choose words from list 1 to go in the boxes and from list 2 to go in the bubbles.

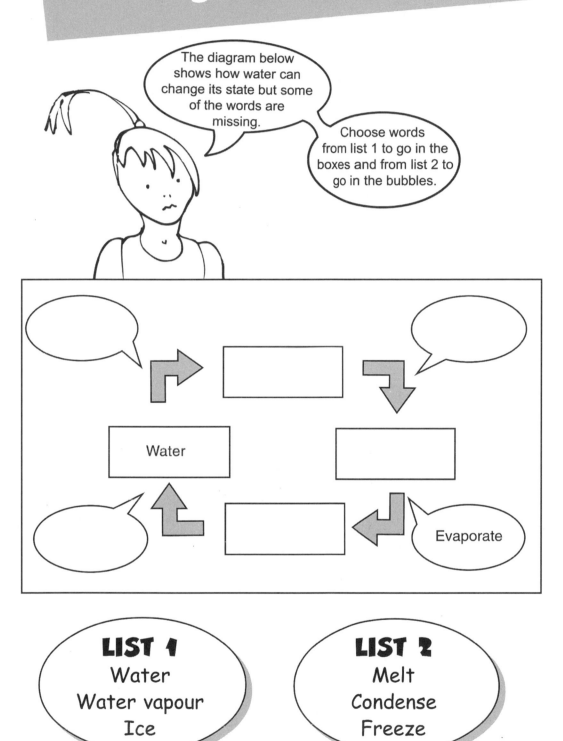

Energy Transfer

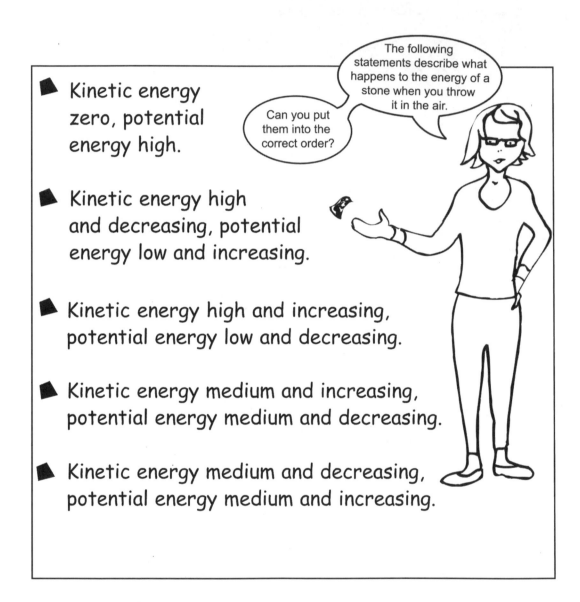

- Kinetic energy zero, potential energy high.

- Kinetic energy high and decreasing, potential energy low and increasing.

- Kinetic energy high and increasing, potential energy low and decreasing.

- Kinetic energy medium and increasing, potential energy medium and decreasing.

- Kinetic energy medium and decreasing, potential energy medium and increasing.

The following statements describe what happens to the energy of a stone when you throw it in the air.

Can you put them into the correct order?

Thought experiments

What is a thought experiment?

A thought experiment is a prediction about what is likely to happen in a situation where it would not be easy to carry out a real-life experiment. They lend themselves to situations such as large scale changes (e.g. movement of the planets), small scale changes (e.g. particle theory), long term changes (e.g. ecological or geological change) or working with potentially dangerous substances. It may be possible to find out through research what happens if other people carry out the experiment.

How can you use thought experiments?

Thought experiments can be useful at the start of a topic as a way of getting learners thinking about the topic. As they go on to investigate and research they can obtain more information which helps to confirm or modify their ideas about the thought experiment. They are also useful part way through or at the end of a topic as a way of getting learners to apply their learning in a new situation. They can be presented through pictures, text, simulation, discussion or a combination of these. They can lead to discussion or they may go further and produce a tangible outcome, such as a diagram or writing.

Thought experiments can be an individual or a group activity. As an individual activity they can give you access to the learners' individual ideas. As a group activity they provide a basis for debate and scientific argument as learners share their ideas within the group.

> **Thought experiments offer an opportunity for learners to think creatively in science lessons.**

How can thought experiments help with assessment?

The predicted outcomes of the thought experiments give you access to the learners' ideas, which you can use for assessment. This can be particularly useful in areas which it is not possible to address by hands-on investigation. Asking learners to explain and give reasons for their predictions provides further information about their thinking. It is possible to create thought experiments to target potential misconceptions and to obtain specific information about how learners are thinking.

How can thought experiments help with learning?

Thought experiments offer an opportunity for learners to think creatively in science lessons without being constrained by the resources available to them. They can be a motivating stimulus which promotes thinking and talking about science in order to solve problems. They generate the need for research to clarify some of the questions that arise in the thought experiments and they enable learners to review and consolidate their ideas as they apply their ideas in novel situations.

Falling under gravity is based on Nussbaum (1985).

Falling Stone

The picture shows people at different points on the Earth's surface dropping a stone.

Which way do you think the stone will fall for each person? Draw in what you think will happen.

Predator - Prey

THE POPULATION OF RABBITS, BUZZARDS AND FOXES IN THE FIELDS SURROUNDING A WOODLAND HAS BEEN FAIRLY STABLE FOR SOME TIME. THE RABBITS FEED ON SEEDLINGS IN THE FIELD. THE BUZZARDS AND FOXES BOTH EAT RABBITS AS ONE OF THEIR MAIN FOOD SOURCES.

NOW THE FIELDS HAVE BEEN SOLD TO A NEW FARMER WHO PLANS TO KEEP CHICKENS AND TO GROW LETTUCE IN THE FIELDS. THE NEW FARMER PLANS TO LAY TRAPS FOR THE FOXES BECAUSE THE FOXES MIGHT ATTACK AND EAT THE CHICKENS.

◆ What do you predict will happen to the population of buzzards over the next two years?

◆ Why do you think the buzzard population might be affected?

◆ Predict any other changes that might happen.

◆ Will the farmer be successful in growing lettuce? What do you think? Explain your answer.

© S Naylor, B Keogh, A Goldsworthy (2004)

True-False statements

What are True-False statements?

True-False statements are simple statements that learners classify as either True or False. With older learners you may decide to add a third category of "It all depends on . . ." or, "I'm not sure because . . ." or, "still thinking" for when they want to qualify their answer.

How can you use True-False statements?

The format that you use will depend on the age and maturity of the learners and how fluent they are as readers. You can type out the statements and copy them as a handout for each learner or group. You can display them on an overhead projector, board or flip chart. You can read them out, though that tends to be less effective as it limits the learners to talking about one statement at a time. You can type them out and include a picture linked to each statement to support less fluent readers.

How can True-False statements help with assessment?

If you use True-False statements at the end of a topic then they can be extremely valuable for individual summative assessment. Although the format is quick and simple they provide a surprising amount of assessment information.

However, that doesn't have much impact on learning. It is more productive to use them for formative assessment with groups at the beginning of a new topic or area of work. Ask each group to discuss the statements, try to agree on what they think and to be clear about any points of disagreement. After sufficient

139

time for discussion get each group to feedback to the whole class. As they feedback you will be able to identify which statements they all agree with and where there are areas of disagreement or uncertainty. These areas of disagreement or uncertainty should then be the focus for the next activity, in which the learners need to find out more about these areas. Usually where there is complete agreement the learners understand the answer, but there may be times when you want to interject and disagree with the class.

After some sort of enquiry (which can include looking things up in books) or practical investigation the class can be brought together for a plenary. The plenary helps you to identify how their ideas have developed and gives you the opportunity to add to, modify or extend their ideas.

How can True-False statements help with learning?

As the learners discuss their ideas they are likely to change their ideas. Justifying their own ideas, listening to other people's views and discussing what evidence is available is an important aspect of learning in science. Identifying their areas of disagreement or uncertainty sets a learning agenda for the learners. This is a useful way of building on their ideas and developing them further. For example, disagreement about whether an elastic band can push as well as pull can lead to useful work on how to change the direction in which a force acts.

Pushes and Pulls

- Pushes can make things move.

- We can push with our legs but we can't pull with them.

- We usually open a cupboard door by pushing it.

- We throw a ball by pushing it quickly.

- An elastic band can push as well as pull.

- Pushing is harder work than pulling.

- In a tug of war one team pulls and the other team pushes.

- A spring can pull but it can't push.

Are the following statements true or false? What do you think?

Earth and Beyond

- Day and night are caused by the Earth spinning on its axis.

- The Earth goes round the Sun every 24 hours.

- The Moon reflects light from the Sun.

- The Earth reflects light from the Sun.

- The Sun is further away from the Earth during the winter.

- Lunar eclipses are more frequent than solar eclipses.

- One half of the Moon is in constant darkness.

- The Earth rotates anti-clockwise.

Are the following statements true or false? What do you think?

142

Word definitions

What are word definitions?

Word definitions describe the learners' own understanding of the words that they will meet in science.

How can you use word definitions?

Different learners will have different definitions and will express them in different ways. Ideally, definitions should be as clear and concise as possible. Key words can usually be categorised into one of three categories: names (e.g. stamen, vein), processes (e.g. melting, fertilisation) or concepts (e.g. force, fruit).

You can ask learners to consider word definitions at several points in a unit of work but they are especially useful at the beginning and end of a unit or section of work. This way the learners can note any changes to the definitions and can discuss how their understanding of the word has improved. Some learners may need reassurance that they are not expected to 'know the answer' at the start of a unit and that some words may be new to them. You can encourage them to offer some response. It may be helpful to have a column where learners can say how sure they are about their definitions. If learners compare and discuss responses with their partner or in a small group they will encounter different viewpoints. This in turn will help them to formulate their own ideas.

One possible approach is to suggest that learners produce their word definitions for someone else who has no knowledge of the word in question, such as a child learning our language, a younger pupil or a visitor from outer space. This helps to create a sense of purpose for generating definitions.

How can word definitions help with assessment?

The word definitions that learners produce give you access to information that you can use for assessment. The clarity, accuracy and complexity of the definitions give a good indication of the learners' level of understanding. Although definitions might appear to be a very small aspect of what learners understand, in reality they can act as important indicators of the level of understanding reached.

How can word definitions help with learning?

Thinking about the words they use can help learners clarify their ideas. For example, a learner might start by saying that condensation is the wet stuff you get on windows in cold weather and finish by saying that it is when a material in its gas state changes into its liquid state. Recognising how their definitions have changed can be a useful way of helping learners to assess for themselves how much they have learnt. This type of self-assessment increases motivation and reinforces learning. Once learners have defined key words in their own terms, they will be far more likely to use them meaningfully in their writing and speech.

Forces

OUR IDEAS ABOUT KEY WORDS AT THE START		DATE:
Word	What WE think it means	How sure are WE? *** = Pretty sure ** = Some bits OK * = Not very sure
Force		
Friction		
Newton		
Gravity		
Air resistance		

OUR IDEAS ABOUT KEY WORDS AT THE END		DATE:
Word	What WE think it means	How sure are WE? *** = Pretty sure ** = Some bits OK * = Not very sure
Force		
Friction		
Newton		
Gravity		
Air resistance		

145

Food Chains

© S Naylor, B Keogh, A Goldsworthy (2004)

OUR IDEAS ABOUT KEY WORDS AT THE START		DATE:
Word	What WE think it means	How sure are WE? *** = Pretty sure ** = Some bits OK * = Not very sure
Consumer		
Producer		
Predator		
Prey		
Food chain		

OUR IDEAS ABOUT KEY WORDS AT THE END		DATE:
Word	What WE think it means	How sure are WE? *** = Pretty sure ** = Some bits OK * = Not very sure
Consumer		
Producer		
Predator		
Prey		
Food chain		

PART 3

References and bibliography 149

Related titles of interest 151

References and bibliography

Adamczyk, P., Willson, M. and Williams, D. (1994) Concept mapping: a multi-level and multi-purpose tool. School Science Review, 76, 275, 118-124.

Assessment Reform Group (1999) Assessment for learning: beyond the black box. Cambridge: University of Cambridge.

Black, P. and Wiliam, D. (1998) Inside the black box. London: Kings College.

Black, P., Harrison, C., Lee, C., Marshall, B. and Wiliam, D. (2002) Working inside the black box. London: Kings College.

Burton, N. (1995) How to be brilliant at recording in science. Leamington Spa: Brilliant Publications.

Feasey, R. (1999) Primary science and literacy links. Hatfield: Association for Science Education.

Fawcett, M. (1998) Business plans from classroom ideas. Primary Science Review, 54, 12-13.

Harlen, W. (2000) The teaching of science in primary schools (3rd Edition). London: David Fulton.

Naylor, S. and Keogh, B. (2000) Concept cartoons in science education. Sandbach: Millgate House.

Nuffield Primary Science (1993). Nuffield Primary Science Teachers' Guides (various titles). London, Collins Educational.

Nussbaum, J. (1985) The Earth as a cosmic body. In R.Driver, E.Guesne and A.Tiberghien (Eds) Children's ideas in science (p.170-192). Milton Keynes: Open University.

SATIS (1992) Frogs, toads and turtles. SATIS 8-14, Box 2, Book 3. Hatfield: ASE.

Sizmur, S. (1994) Concept mapping, language and learning in the classroom. School Science Review, 76, 274, 120-125.

Swartz, R., Larisey, J. and Kiser, M.A. (2000) Infusion lessons: teaching critical and creative thinking in language arts. Pacific Grove: Critical Thinking Books & Software. (Also see www.criticalthinking.com)

White, R. and Gunstone, R. (1992) Probing understanding. London: Falmer Press.

Related titles of interest

Starting Points for Science
Brenda Keogh and Stuart Naylor (1997)
ISBN   0 9527506 1 9

Concept Cartoons In Science Education (Book version)
Stuart Naylor and Brenda Keogh (2000)
ISBN   0 9527506 2 7

Concept Cartoons In Science Education (CD ROM version)
Stuart Naylor and Brenda Keogh (2000)

Thinking About Science posters (set of 20)
Brenda Keogh and Stuart Naylor (1999)

The Science Questions book series is published by Hodder Children's Books
and obtainable from Millgate House Publishers

The Snowman's Coat and other science questions
Brenda and Stuart Naylor (2000)
ISBN 0340 757558

The Snowman's Coat and other science questions (Big book)
Brenda and Stuart Naylor (2000)
ISBN 0340 77925X

The Seesaw and other science questions
Brenda and Stuart Naylor (2000)
ISBN 0340 764430

<u>Upside Down Seeds and other science questions</u>
Brenda and Stuart Naylor (2000)
ISBN 0340 764457

<u>Bungee Jumpers and other science questions</u>
Brenda and Stuart Naylor (2000)
ISBN 0340 764414

For enquiries about these books or about consultancy/professional development contact:

Millgate House Publishing and Consultancy
Tel/Fax +44(0)1270 764314
Email enquiries@millgatehouse.co.uk
www.millgatehouse.co.uk

From David Fulton Publishers:

<u>The Teaching of Science in Primary Schools</u> (Fourth edition, 2004)
By Wynne Harlen OBE and Anne Qualter
ISBN 1 84312 132 8

<u>Challenges in Primary Science: Meeting the Needs of Able</u>
<u>Young Scientists at Key Stage Two</u> (2003)
By David Coates and Helen Wilson
ISBN 1 84312 013 5

<u>Science and ICT in the Primary School:</u>
<u>A Creative Approach to Big Ideas</u> (2004)
By John Meadows
ISBN 1 84312 120 4

<u>Using Science to Develop Thinking Skills at Key Stage 1</u> (2004)
By Max de Boo
ISBN 1 84312 150 6

<u>Using Science to Develop Thinking Skills at Key Stage:</u>
<u>Materials for Gifted Children</u> (2003)
By Pat O'Brien
ISBN 1 84312 037 3

To order call David Fulton Publishers on 020 8996 3610